The Aleph Bet Coloring Book

All rights are reserved by Michelle Geft, and any content of this book may not be reproduced, downloaded, disseminated, published, or transferred in any form or by any means, except with the prior written permission of Michelle Geft.

Published by Hebrew Basics
© 2017 Michelle Geft
All rights reserved
Manufactured in the United States of America
ISBN-13 978-0-9991405-1-2

This book has an online companion at: www.HebrewBasics.com (See QR code below). You have free access to videos and downloadable pdfs to help explain the letters, vowels, the "ch" /"h" sound, the sofit (end) letters and so much more. You will also find links to games and quizzes to help you learn.

Note to educators:
Please contact me directly for discounted bulk orders.

hebrewbasics.com

VOWELS:

The vowels in Hebrew are small symbols found under, above or to the left of the letter. You will find the vowels on the left of this page. On the right, we are using the letter *Aleph* (א) as a sample of how the vowel looks when combined with a letter. The letter *Aleph* is a silent letter, so it simply adopts the sound of the vowel.

↓ Vowels   Vowels with a letter ↓

Vowel	Description	Letter
ָ	The *Kamatz* says "ah" as in <u>A</u>qua.	אָ
ַ	The *Pata<u>h</u>* says "ah" as in <u>A</u>qua.	אַ
ֶ	The *Segol* says "eh" as in <u>R</u>ed.	אֶ
ֵ	The *Tzeireh* says "eh"(ay) as in <u>R</u>ed.	אֵ
ִ	The *Heerik* says "ee" as in Gr<u>ee</u>n.	אִ
וֹ	The *Holam* says "o" as in <u>O</u>range.	אוֹ
ֹ	The *Holam* says "o" as in <u>O</u>range.	אֹ
וּ	The *Kubootz* says "oo" as in Bl<u>ue</u>.	אוּ
ֻ	The *Shurook* says "oo" as in Bl<u>ue</u>.	אֻ
ְ	The *Shva* says "ih" as in <u>I</u>ndigo.*	אְ

*The Shva is not technically a vowel, but for purposes of this book we will introduce it in this way. It is rarely used with an Aleph but for visual purposes only, I used it here. The Shva sometimes silent.

2   The Aleph Bet Coloring Book © 2017 Michelle Geft

READING:

You read Hebrew from right to left. When you read each letter with a vowel, you read it by combining the sound the letter makes with the sound of the vowel it is paired with. First you say the sound of the letter then you add the sound of the vowel. The *Aleph* adopts the sound of the vowel because it is a silent letter. If we use the example of the letter *Bet* (בּ) that makes the sound B' as in boy, we read it like this:

Read below from left to right.

b (בּ) + ah (ָ) = bah **/** Bah = בָּ

b (בּ) + ah (ַ) = bah **/** Bah = בַּ

b (בּ) + eh (ֵ) = beh **/** Beh = בֵּ

b (בּ) + eh (ֶ) = beh **/** Beh = בֶּ

b (בּ) + ee (ִ) = bee **/** Bee = בִּ

b (בּ) + o (ֹ) = bo **/** Bo = בֹּ

b (בּ) + o (וֹ) = bo **/** Bo = בוֹ

b (בּ) + oo (ֻ) = boo **/** Boo = בֻּ

b (בּ) + oo (וּ) = boo **/** Boo = בוּ

b (בּ) + ih (ְ) = bih **/** Bih = בְּ

NOTE: This book is intended to introduce you to the Hebrew alphabet and the vowels. The Hebrew alphabet is called the *Aleph Bet*. There are more rules and exceptions that you will learn if you continue to study. For now, have fun learning!

3   The Aleph Bet Coloring Book © 2017 Michelle Geft

DIRECTIONS FOR BEST USE OF THIS BOOK:

ah
ָ

ah
ַ

eh
ֱ

eh
ֵ

ee
ִ

oh
וֹ

·

oh

oo
וּ

oo
ֻ

ih
ְ

- Use the last page in this book to help you read (page 39). Cut out a "bookmark" and put it to the left of the coloring book as you try to read. There are a few of them, so don't worry if you lose one.
- When you see the star symbol ✡ in the book, please visit www.HebrewBasics.com for an audio/visual companion.
- Here is a hint to reading: Use the sound the letter makes and add the sound of the vowel. For example:

The letter *Gimmel* (גּ) says g' like girl.

גָ says "gah"

גַ says "gah"

גֱ says "geh"

גֵ says "geh"

גִ says "gee"

גוֹ says "go"

גֹ says "go"

גוּ says "goo"

גֻ says "goo" (just like גוּ)

גְ says "gih"

- Please visit www.HebrewBasics.com to learn about the H sound in Hebrew.

4   The Aleph Bet Coloring Book © 2017 Michelle Geft

א בב ג ד ה ו ז ח ט י כך ל מם נן ס ע פף צץ ק ר שש ת

THIS IS THE LETTER ALEPH.
ALEPH IS A SILENT LETTER.

The letter *Aleph* represents the number one.

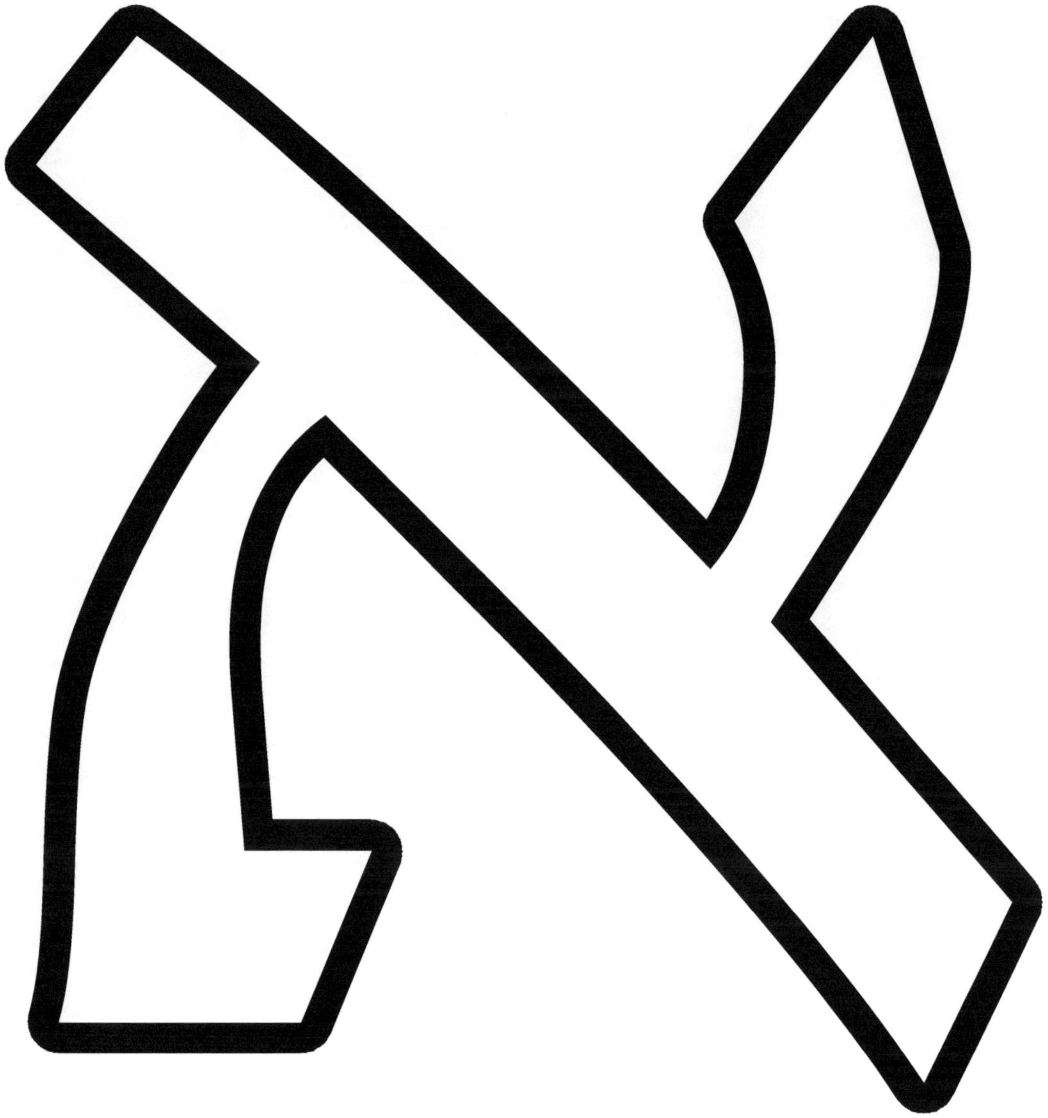

ALEPH

5 The Aleph Bet Coloring Book © 2017 Michelle Geft

אבב ג ד ה ה ו ז ח ח ט י כךך ל ל מם ן ן ס ע פףף צץ ק ר ש ש ת

THIS IS THE LETTER BET.
BET SAYS "B" AS IN BOY.
Notice the dot in the letter,
it is called a *dagesh*.

The letter *Bet* represents the number two.

בְּ

בַּ

בֵּ

בִּ

בֹּ

בֹּי

בֻּ

בְּ

| BET |

6   The Aleph Bet Coloring Book © 2017 Michelle Geft

א בּב ג ד ה ו ז ח ט י כך ל מם נן ס ע פף צץ ק ר שׂשׁ ת

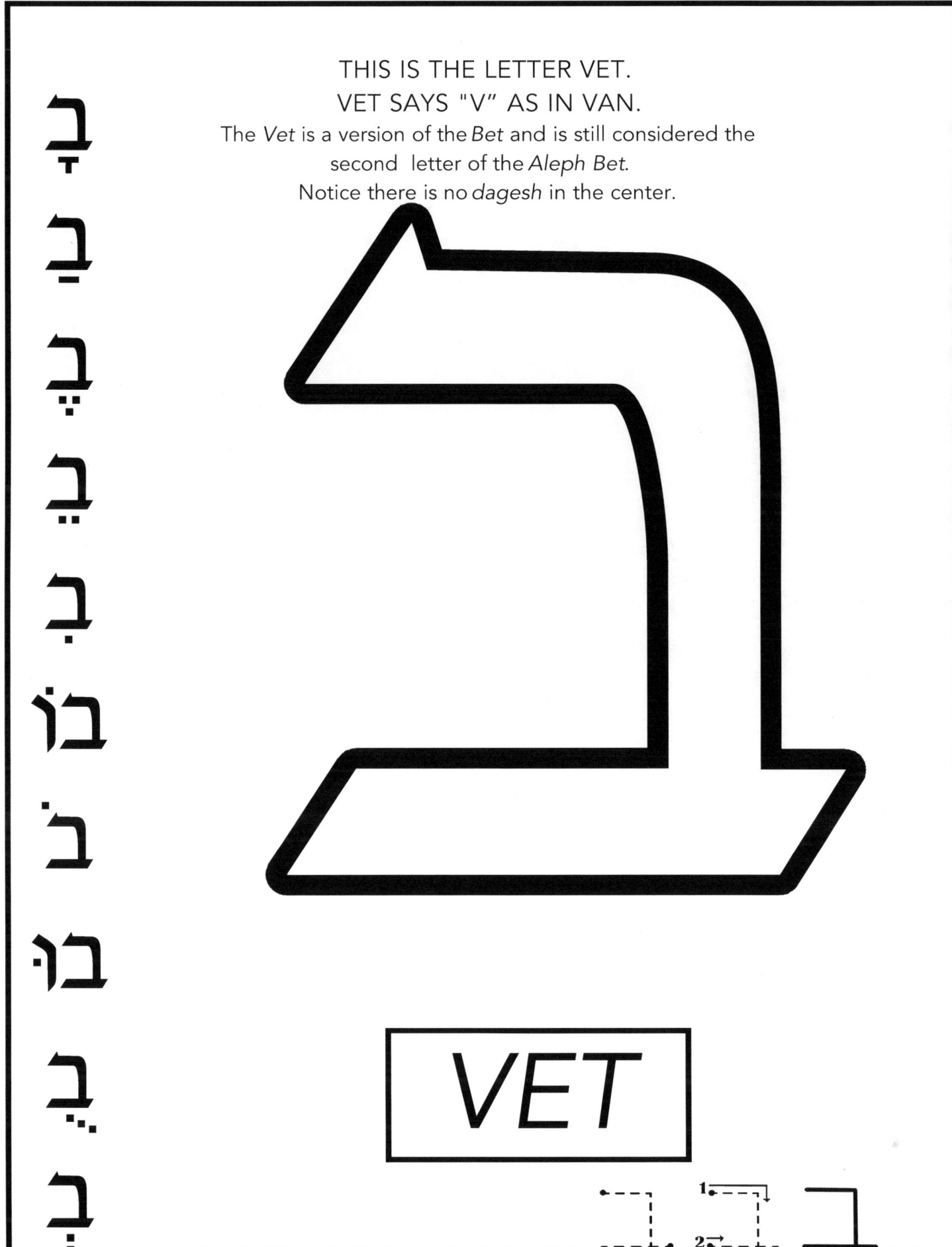

THIS IS THE LETTER VET.
VET SAYS "V" AS IN VAN.

The *Vet* is a version of the *Bet* and is still considered the
second letter of the *Aleph Bet*.
Notice there is no *dagesh* in the center.

VET

בְּ בֵּ בֶּ בִּ בֹּ בֻּ בֹּ בֵּ בִּ בֵּ

אבב ג ד ה ו ז ח ט י כך ל מם נן ס ע פּףּ צץ ק ר שׂשׁ ת

THIS IS THE LETTER GIMMEL.
GIMMEL SAYS "G" AS IN GIRL.

The letter *Gimmel* represents the number three.

GIMMEL

8   The Aleph Bet Coloring Book © 2017 Michelle Geft

אבב ג ד ה ו ז ח ט י כךכ ל מם ןנ ס ע ףפפ ץצ ק ר שׁשׂ ת

THIS IS THE LETTER DALET.
DALET SAYS "D" AS IN DOLL.

The letter *Dalet* represents the number four.

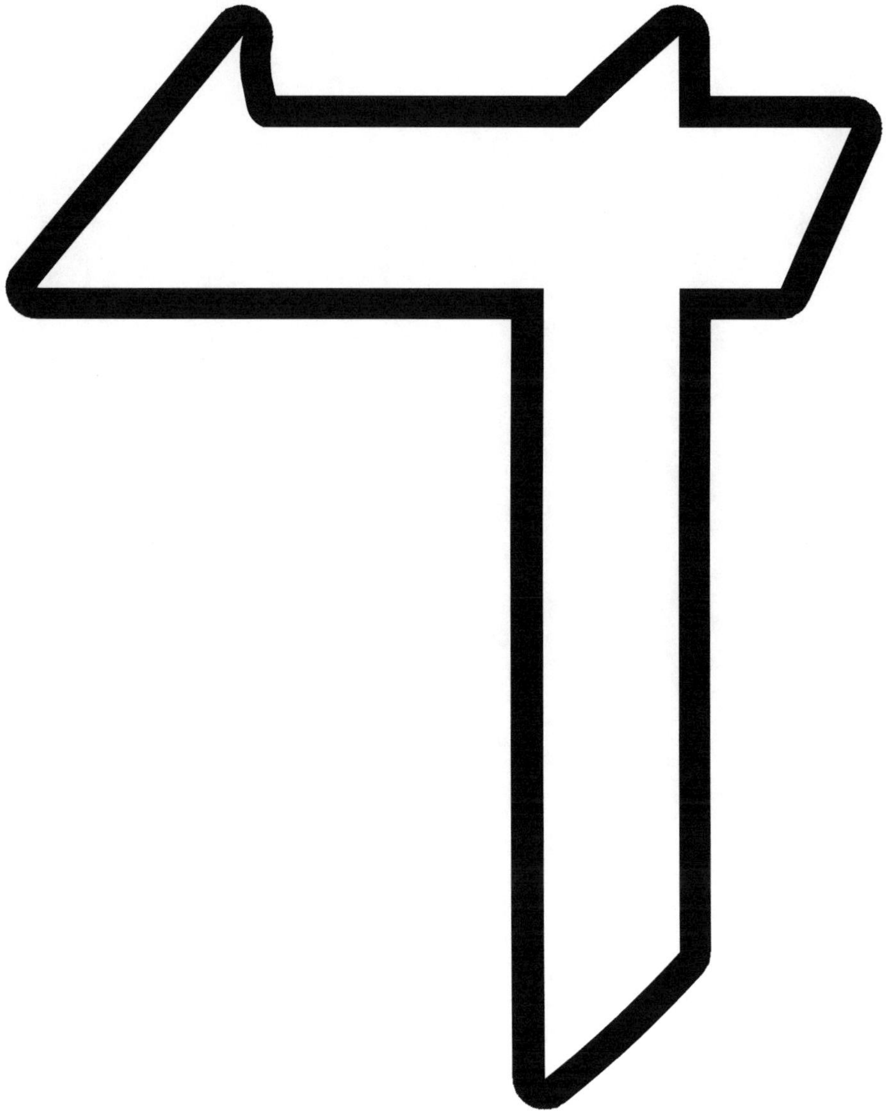

DALET

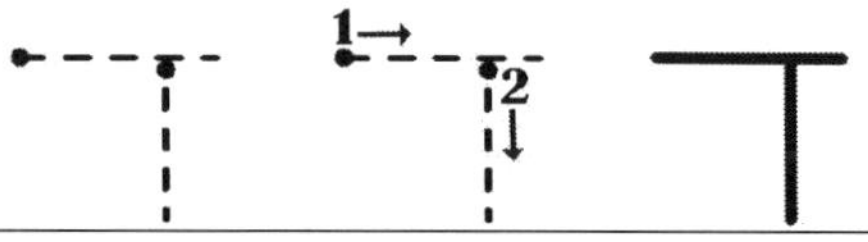

9   The Aleph Bet Coloring Book © 2017 Michelle Geft

אבב ג ד ה ו ז ח ט י ככך ל מס ןן ס ע פפף צץ ק ר שש ת

THIS IS THE LETTER HAY.
HAY SAYS "H" AS IN HAT.

The letter *Hay* represents the number five.

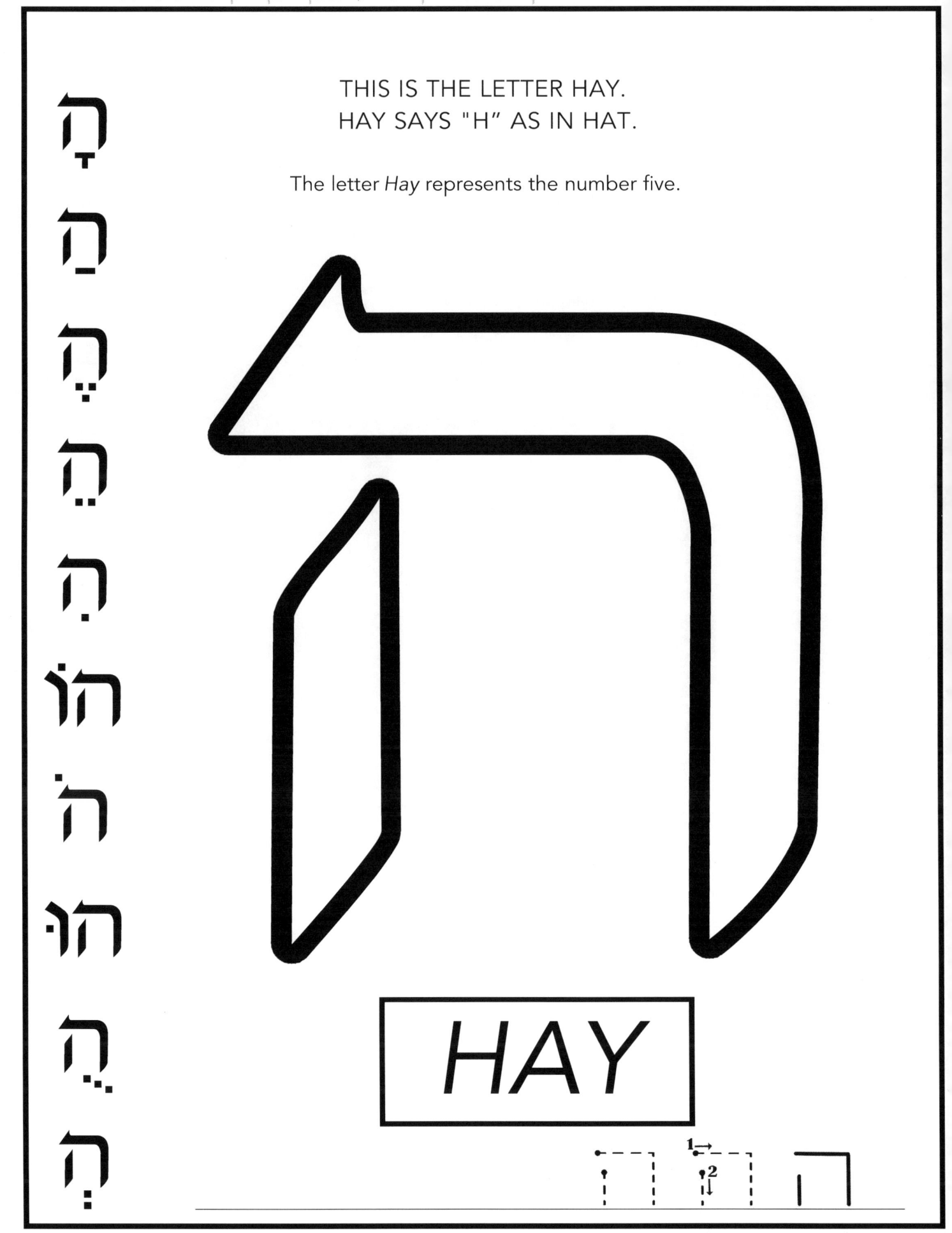

HAY

10   The Aleph Bet Coloring Book © 2017 Michelle Geft

אבב ג ד ה ו ז ח ט י ככך ל מם נן ס ע פפף צץ ק ר שש ת

THIS IS THE LETTER VAV.
VAV SAYS "V" AS IN VINE.
Sometimes *Vav* is used in vowel form and
in that case the *Vav* will be silent. ✡

The letter *Vav* represents the number six.

VAV

11   The Aleph Bet Coloring Book © 2017 Michelle Geft

אבב גד הו ז ח ט י כך ל מם נן ס ע פף ףץ צ ק ר ש ש ת

THIS IS THE LETTER ZAYIN.
ZAYIN SAYS "Z" AS IN ZOO.

The letter *Zayin* represents the number seven.

ZAYIN

12   The Aleph Bet Coloring Book © 2017 Michelle Geft

אבב ג ד ה ו ז ח ט י ככך ל מם נן ס ע פפף צץ ק ר שׂשׁ ת

THIS IS THE LETTER <u>H</u>ET.
<u>H</u>ET SAYS A UNIQUE SOUND
not found in the English language. Similar to how you might
pronounce the German composer's name Bach. Please note
Hebrew does not have the "ch" sound of the word Charlie.
It is a guttoral <u>h</u> sound. ✡

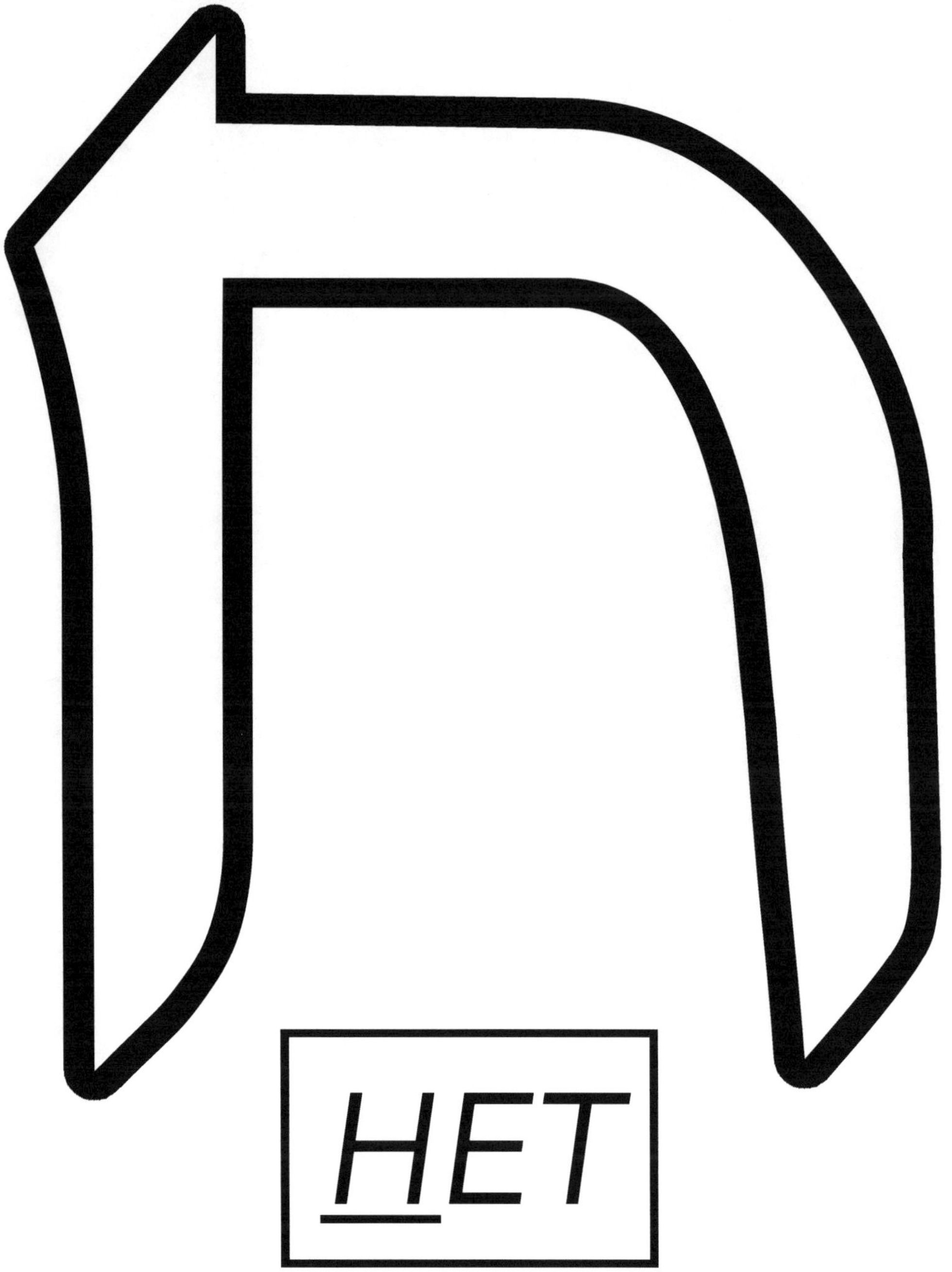

The letter <u>H</u>et represents the number eight.

<u>H</u>ET

13   The Aleph Bet Coloring Book © 2017 Michelle Geft

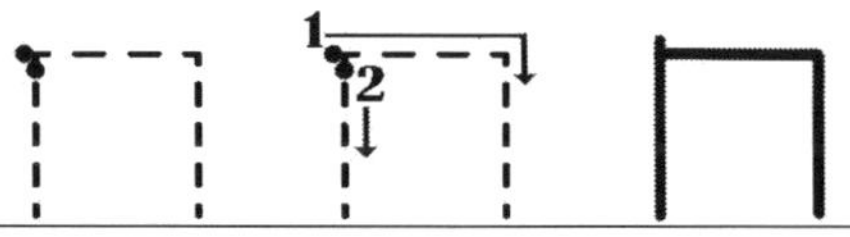

אבב ג ד ה ו ז ח ט י כך ל מם נן ס ע פּפף צץ ק ר שׁשׂ ת

THIS IS THE LETTER TET.
TET SAYS "T" AS IN TIME.

The letter *Tet* represents the number nine.

טָ
טֶ
טֵ
טִ
טֹ
טוֹ
טֻ
טוּ
טְ

TET

א בּב ג ד ה ו ז ח ט י כּכך ל מם נן ס ע פּפף צץ ק ר שׁשׂ ת

THIS IS THE LETTER YUD (YOOD or YOD).
YUD SAYS "Y" AS IN YO-YO.

The letter *Yud* represents the number ten.

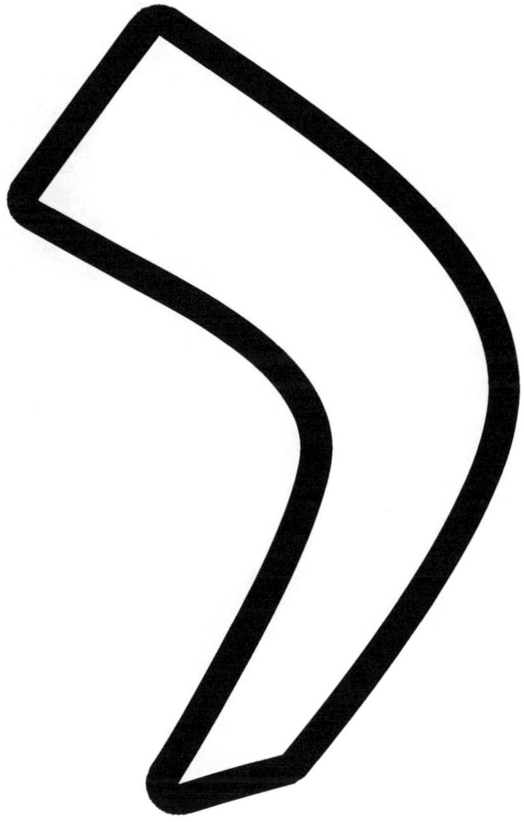

YUD

א בּב ג ד ה ו ז ח ט י כּךכ ל מם נן ס ע פּףפ צץ ק ר שׁשׂ ת

THIS IS THE LETTER KAF.
KAF SAYS "K" AS IN KIND.
You will see in the next couple pages that there are a few
versions of the letter *Kaf*.

The letter *Kaf* represents the number twenty.

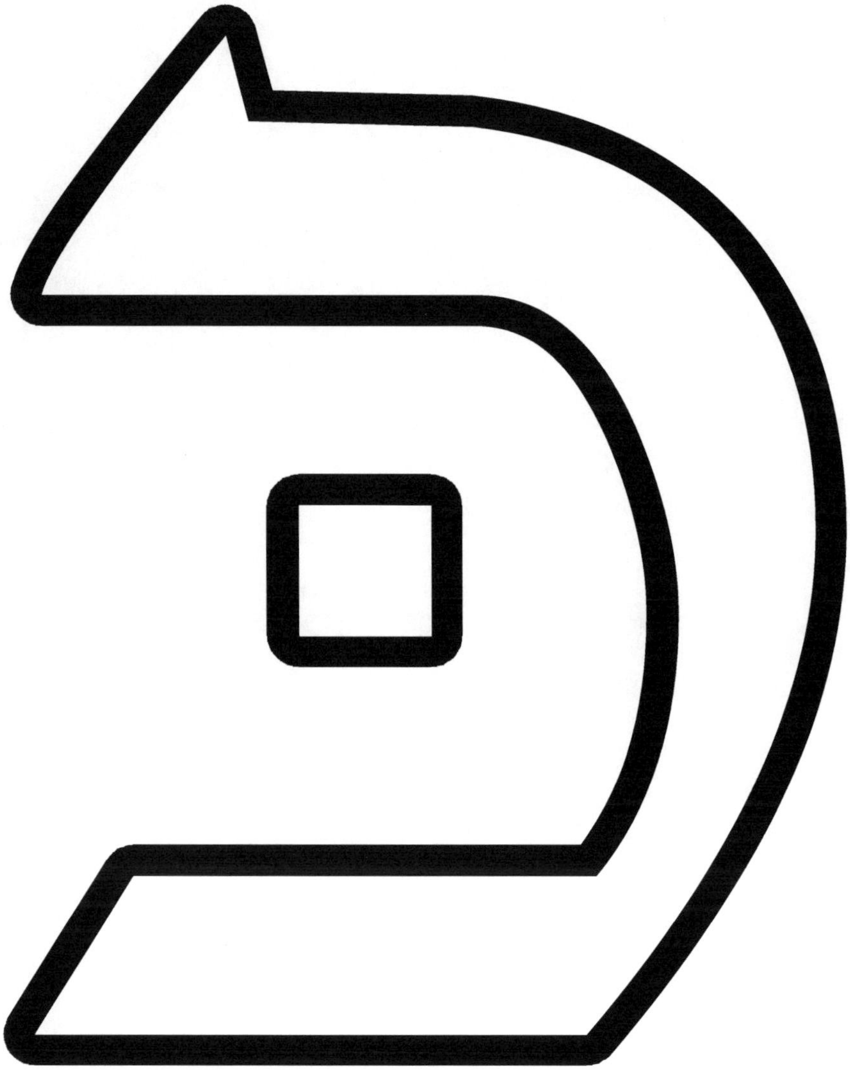

KAF

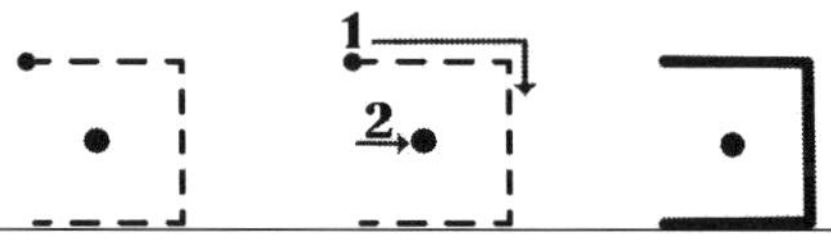

16   The Aleph Bet Coloring Book © 2017 Michelle Geft

א בּב ג ד ה ו ז ח ט י כּךּכך ל מם נן ס ע פּפף צץ ק ר שׁשׂ ת

THIS IS THE LETTER <u>H</u>AF.
<u>H</u>AF SAYS THE SAME SOUND AT <u>H</u>ET.
It is a guttoral "<u>h</u>" sound. <u>H</u>af is a version of the *Kaf*, notice
this one does not have the *dagesh*.

<u>H</u>AF

17   The Aleph Bet Coloring Book © 2017 Michelle Geft

א בב ג ד ה ו ז ח ט י כךכ ל מם ןנ ס ע פףפ צץ ק ר שׁשׂ ת

THIS IS THE LETTER H̲AF SOFIT.
IT USUALLY SAYS "H̲" SOUND, BUT AT TIMES
WILL SAY THE "K" SOUND.
The word "*sofit*" means "end." This letter is found only at
the end of a word and only takes a few vowels. ✡

THE
HAF SOFIT
ONLY TAKES
THESE
VOWELS.

ךֹ

ךְ

SOMETIMES
IN THE
BIBLE AND
IN
LITERATURE,
THE *HAF
SOFIT* GETS
A *DAGESH*
WITH A
KAMATZ
AND THEN
IT SAYS
"KA'"

ךָּ

H̲AF
sofit

18   The Aleph Bet Coloring Book © 2017 Michelle Geft

א בב ג ד ה ו ז ח ט י כך ל מם נן ס ע פף צץ ק ר שש ת

THIS IS THE LETTER LA'MED.
LA'MED SAY "L" AS IN LOVE.

The letter *La'med* represents the number thirty.

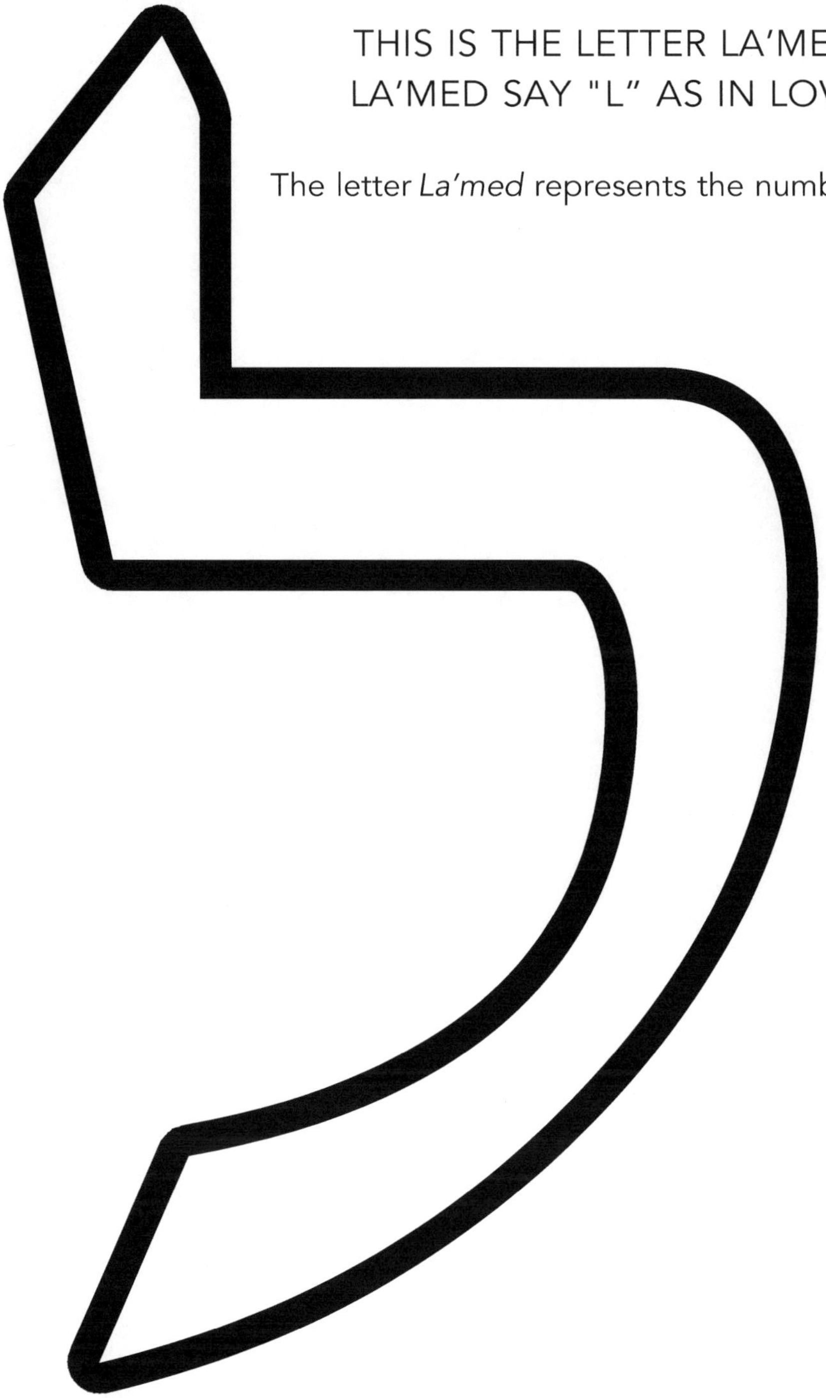

LAMED

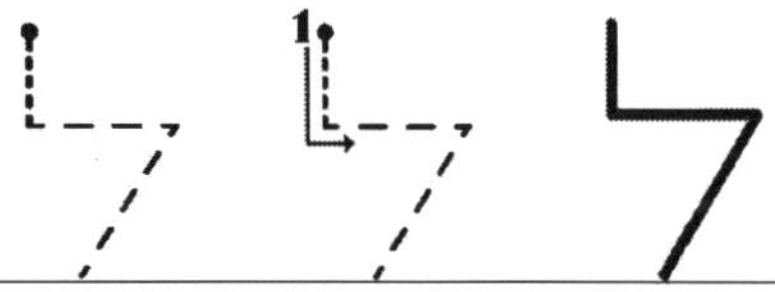

19   The Aleph Bet Coloring Book © 2017 Michelle Geft

א אב ג ד ה ו ז ח ט י כך ל מם נן ס ע פףף צץ ק ר שׁשׂ ת

THIS IS THE LETTER MEM.
MEM SAYS "M" AS IN MOM.

The letter *Mem* represents the number forty.

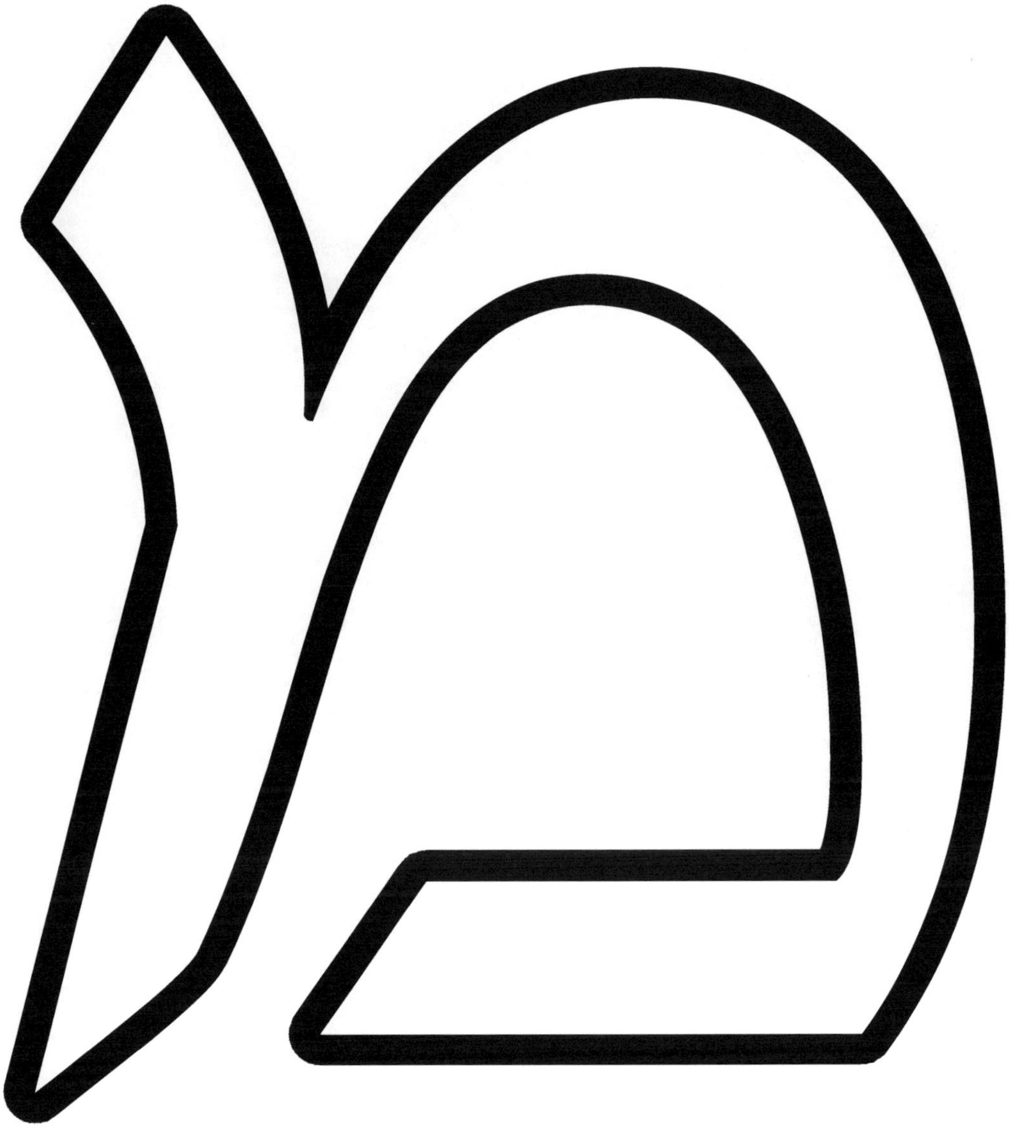

MEM

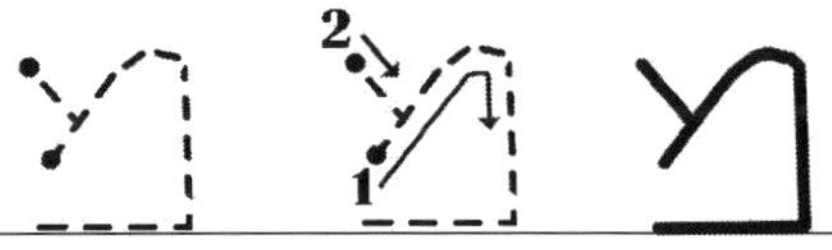

20   The Aleph Bet Coloring Book © 2017 Michelle Geft

א בב ג ד ה ו ז ח ט י כך ל מם נן ס ע פףף צץ ק ר שׁשׁ ת

THIS IS THE LETTER MEM SOFIT.
MEM SOFIT SAYS "M" AS IN MOM.
Mem Sofit is only found at the end of a word
in place of the *Mem*. ✡

THE
MEM SOFIT
DOES NOT
TAKE
VOWELS.

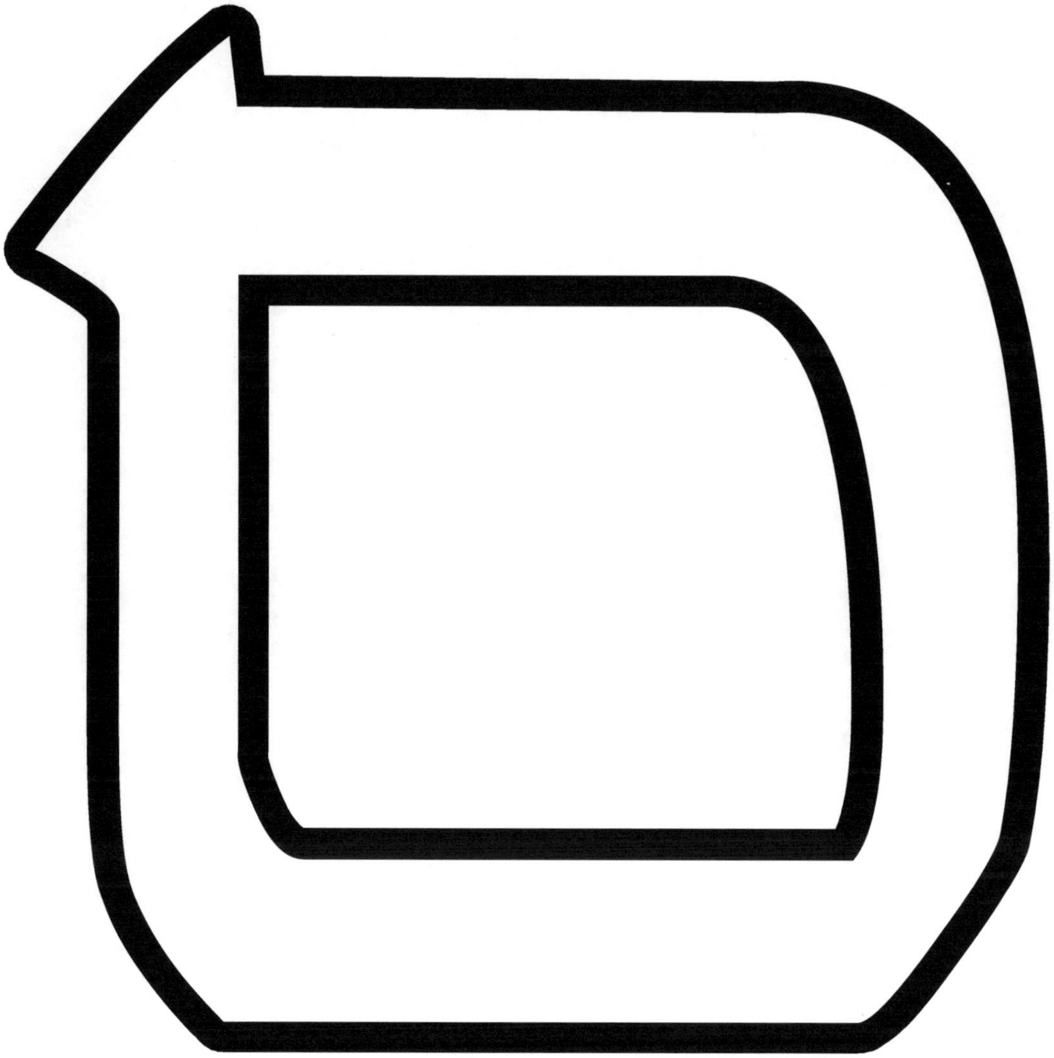

MEM *sofit*

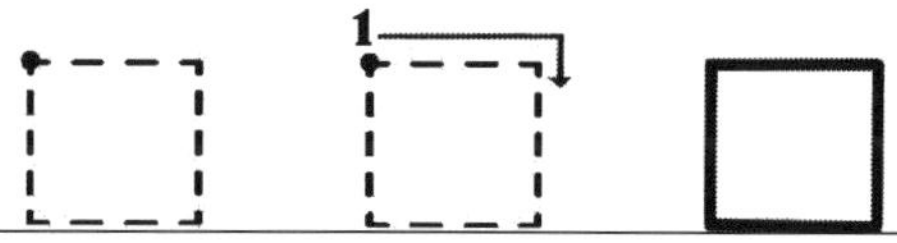

21   The Aleph Bet Coloring Book © 2017 Michelle Geft

אבבג ד ה ו ז ח ט י כך ל מם נן ס ע פף צץ ק ר שׁשׂ ת

THIS IS THE LETTER NUN (NOON).
NUN SAYS "N" AS IN NICE.

The letter *Nun* represents the number fifty.

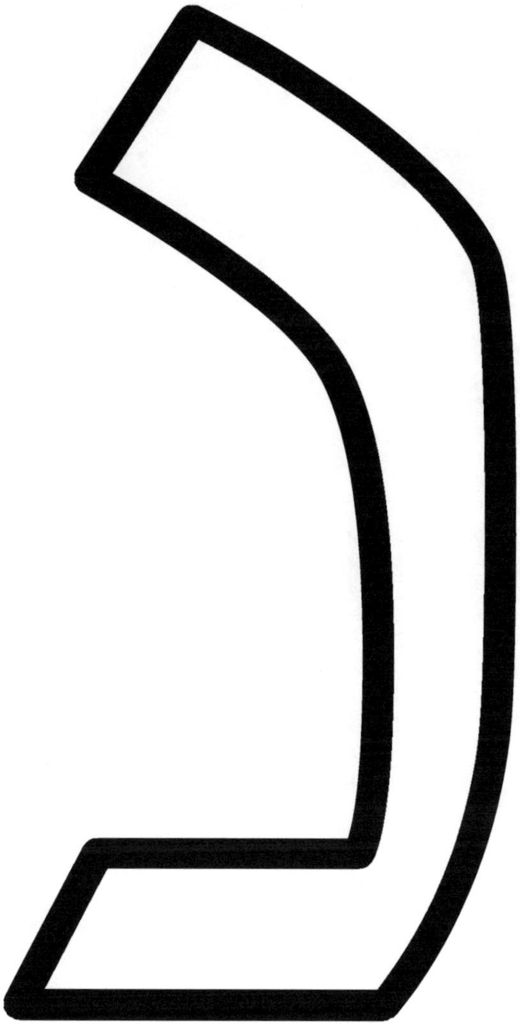

NUN

22   The Aleph Bet Coloring Book © 2017 Michelle Geft

אבב ג ד ה ו ז ח ט י כּכך ל מם ןן ס ע פּפף צץ ק ר שׁשׂ ת

THIS IS THE LETTER NUN SOFIT.
NUN SOFIT SAYS "N" AS IN NICE.
Nun Sofit is only found at the end of a word
in place of the *Nun*. ✡

*THE
NUN SOFIT
DOES NOT
TAKE
VOWELS.*

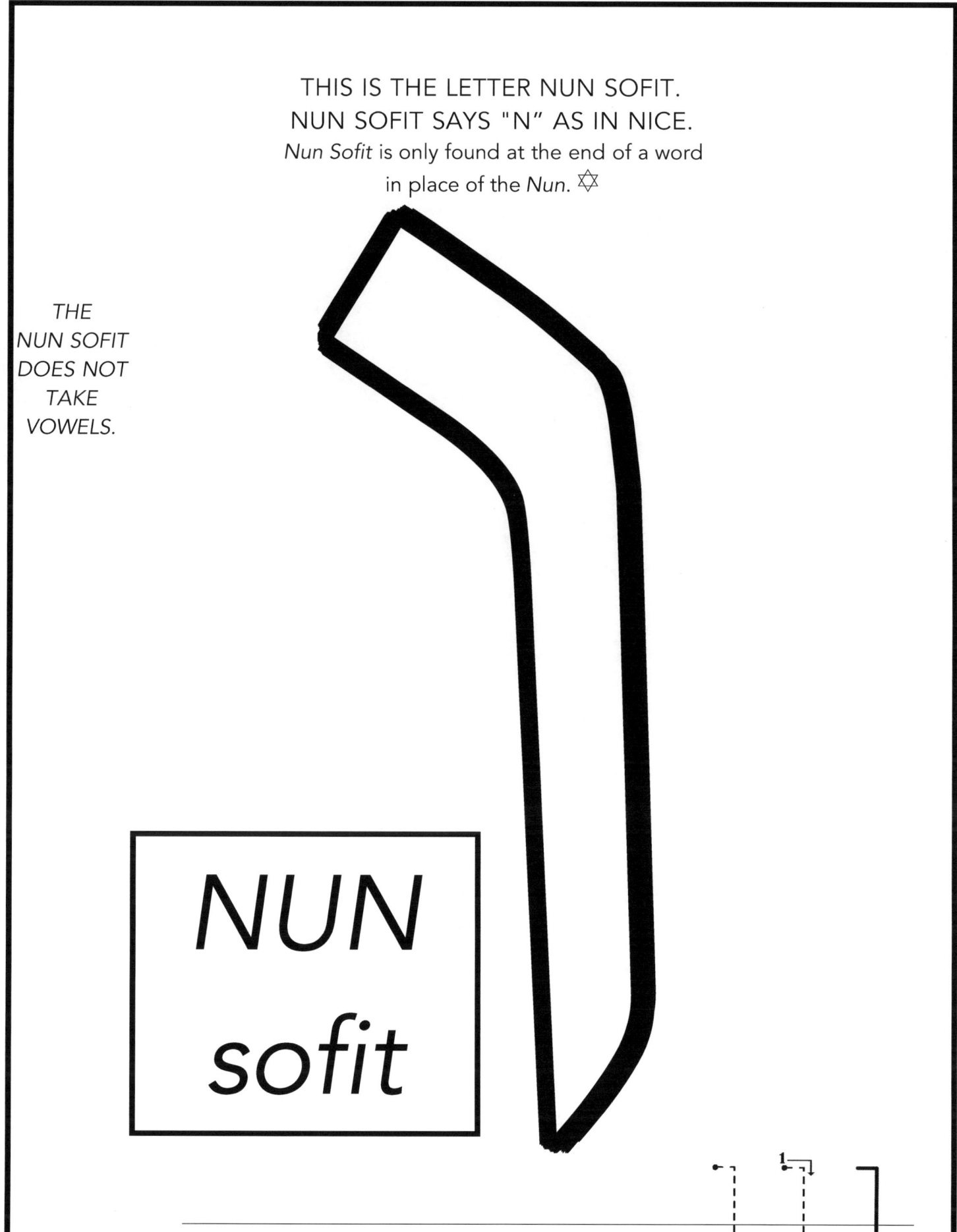

NUN
sofit

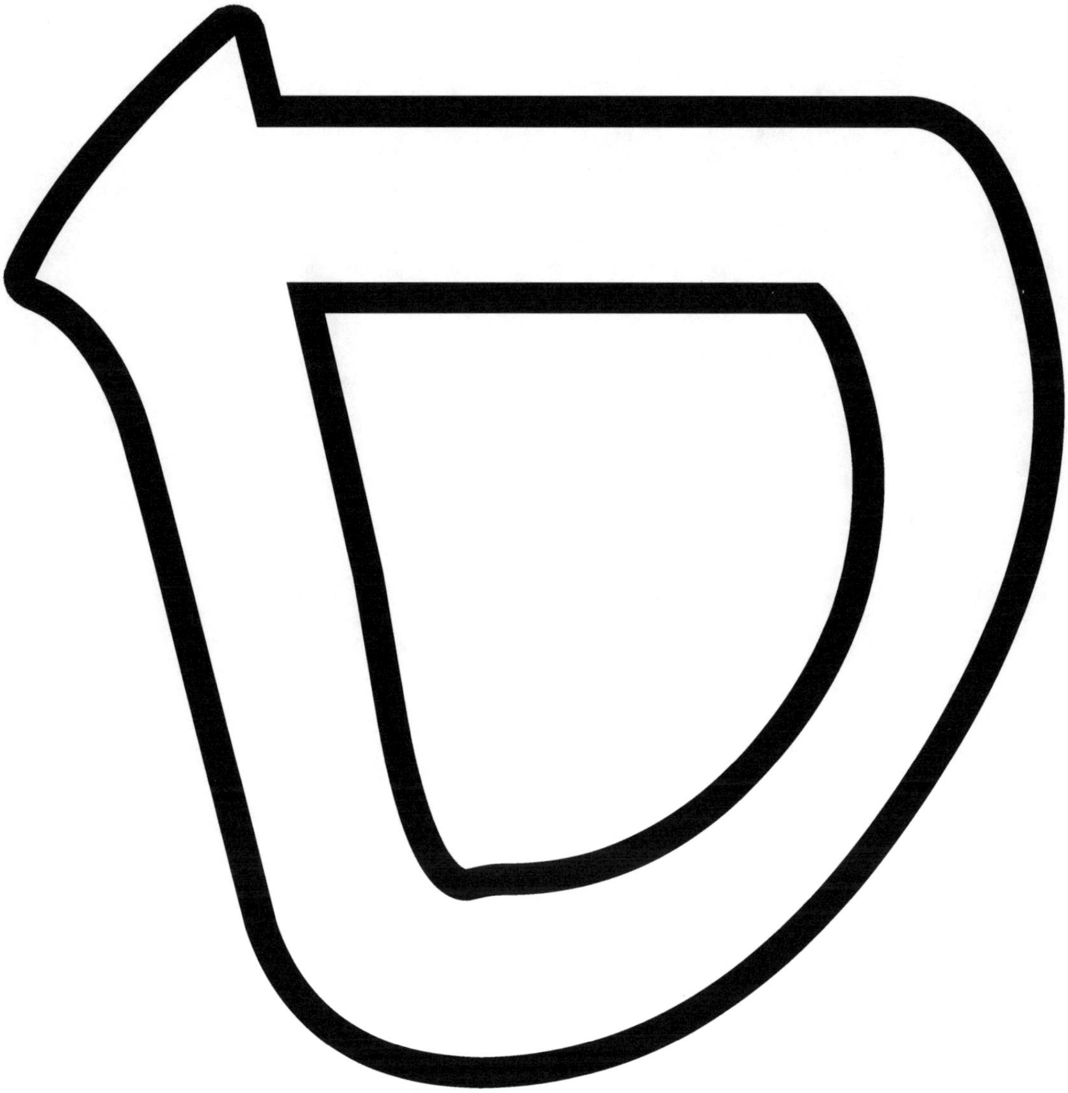

THIS IS THE LETTER SAME_H_.
SAME_H_ SAYS "S" AS IN SUN.

The letter *Sameh* represents the number sixty.

SAME_H_

24   The Aleph Bet Coloring Book © 2017 Michelle Geft

א אב ג ד ה ו ז ח ט י כך ל מם נן ס ע ףפ ץצ ק ר שׁשׁ ת

THIS IS THE LETTER AYIN.
AYIN IS A SILENT LETTER.

The letter *Ayin* represents the number seventy.

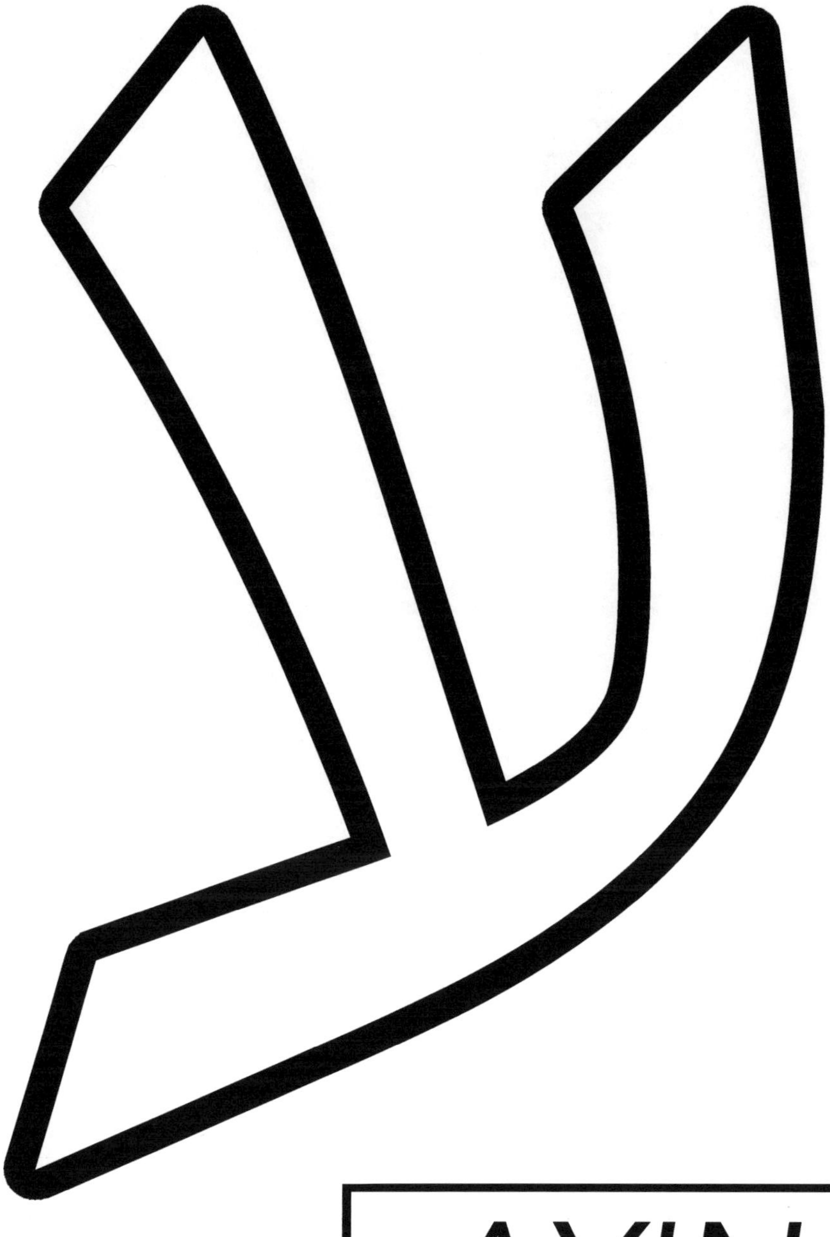

AYIN

25   The Aleph Bet Coloring Book © 2017 Michelle Geft

א בּ ב ג ד ה ו ז ח ט י כּ כ ך ל מ ם נ ן ס ע פּ פ ף צ ץ ק ר שׁ שׂ ת

THIS IS THE LETTER PAY.
PAY SAYS "P" AS IN PEACE.

The letter *Pay* represents the number eighty.

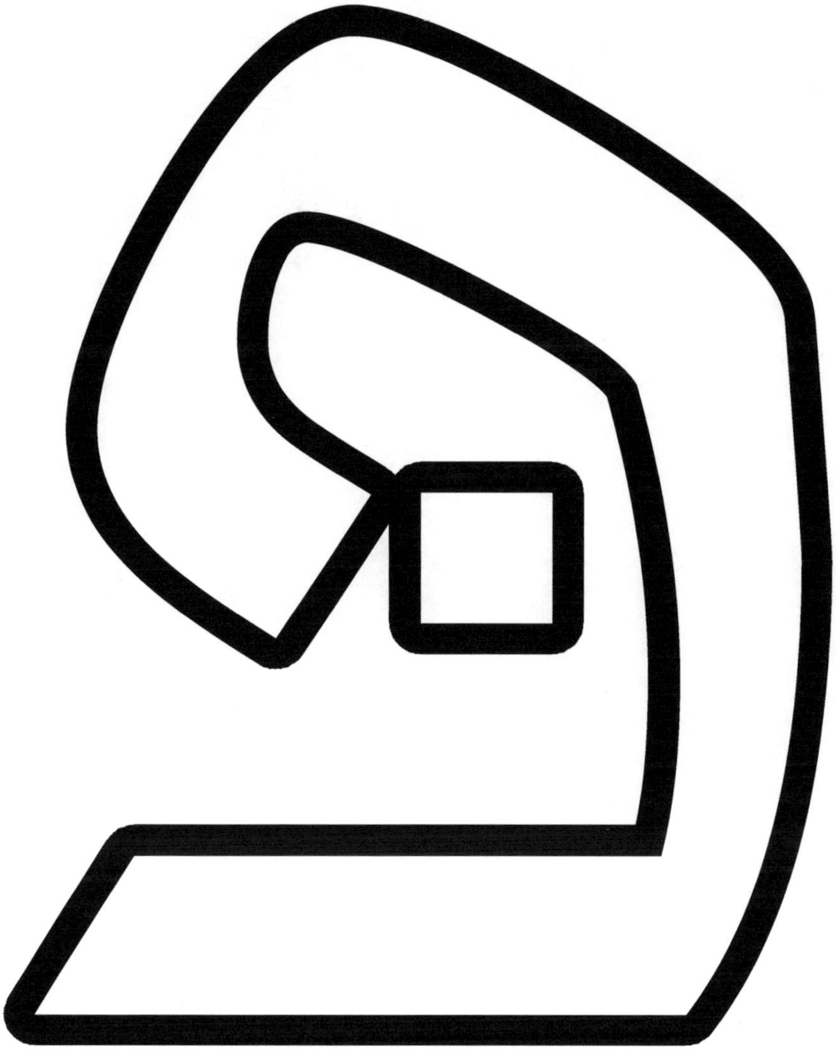

PAY

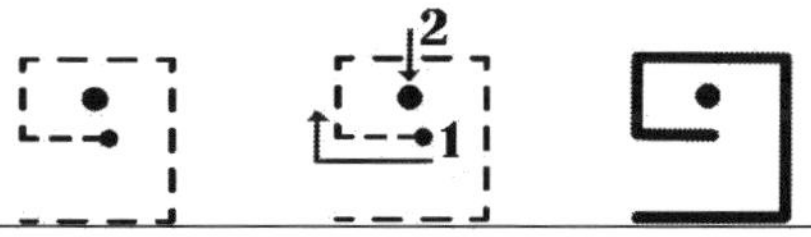

26   The Aleph Bet Coloring Book © 2017 Michelle Geft

א בב ג ד ה ו ז ח ט י כך ל מם נן ס ע פף צץ ק ר שׁשׂ ת

THIS IS THE LETTER FAY.
FAY SAYS "F" AS IN FUN.
The *Fay* is a version of the *Pay*.
Notice there is no *dagesh* in the center.

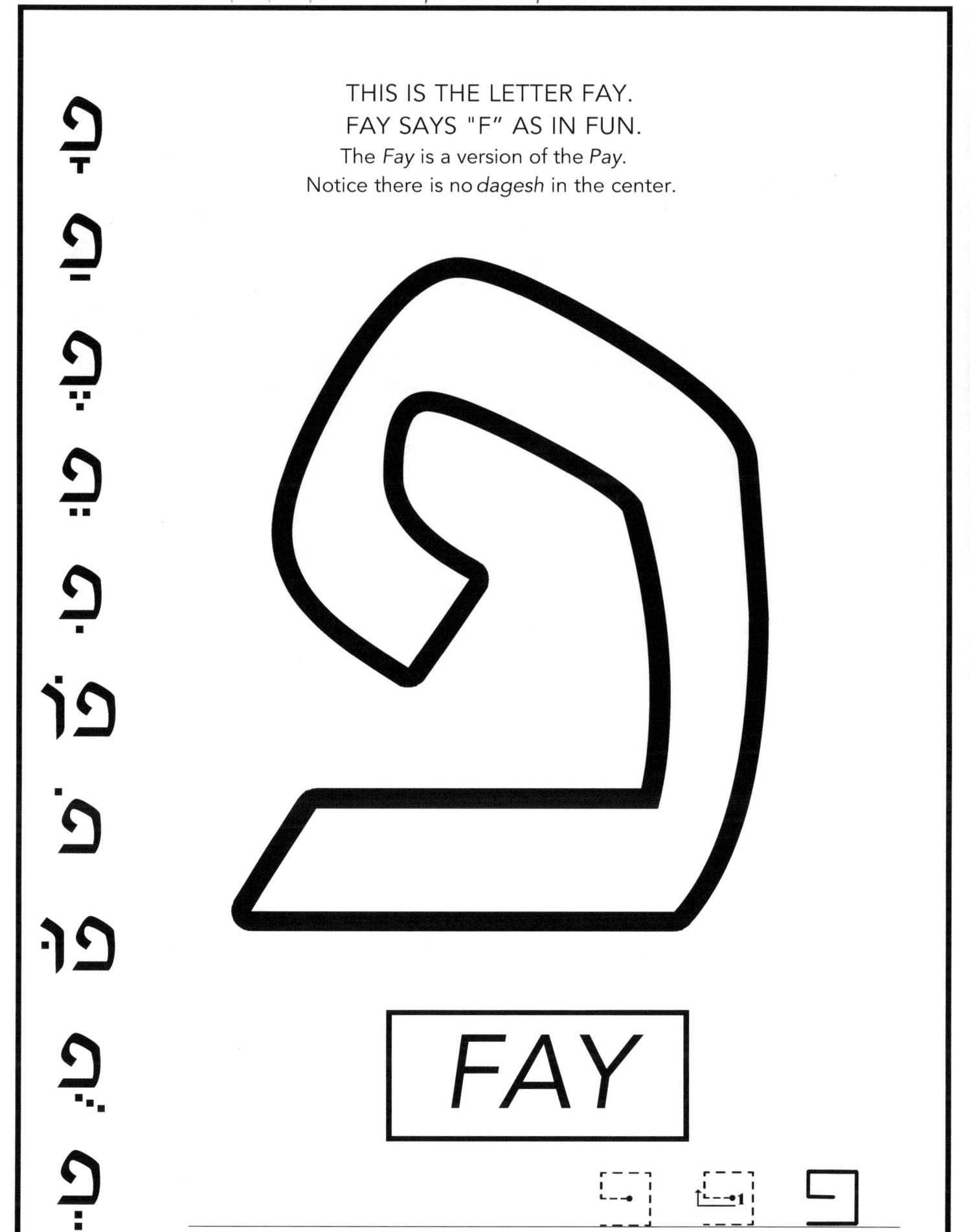

FAY

27 The Aleph Bet Coloring Book © 2017 Michelle Geft

א בּב ג ד ה ו ז ח ט י כּךְ ל מם נן ס ע פּףף צץ ק ר שׁשׂ ת

THIS IS THE LETTER FAY SOFIT.
FAY SOFIT SAYS "F" AS IN FUN.
Fay Sofit is only found at the end of a word
in place of the *Fay.* ✡

THE FAY
SOFIT
DOES NOT
TAKE
VOWELS.

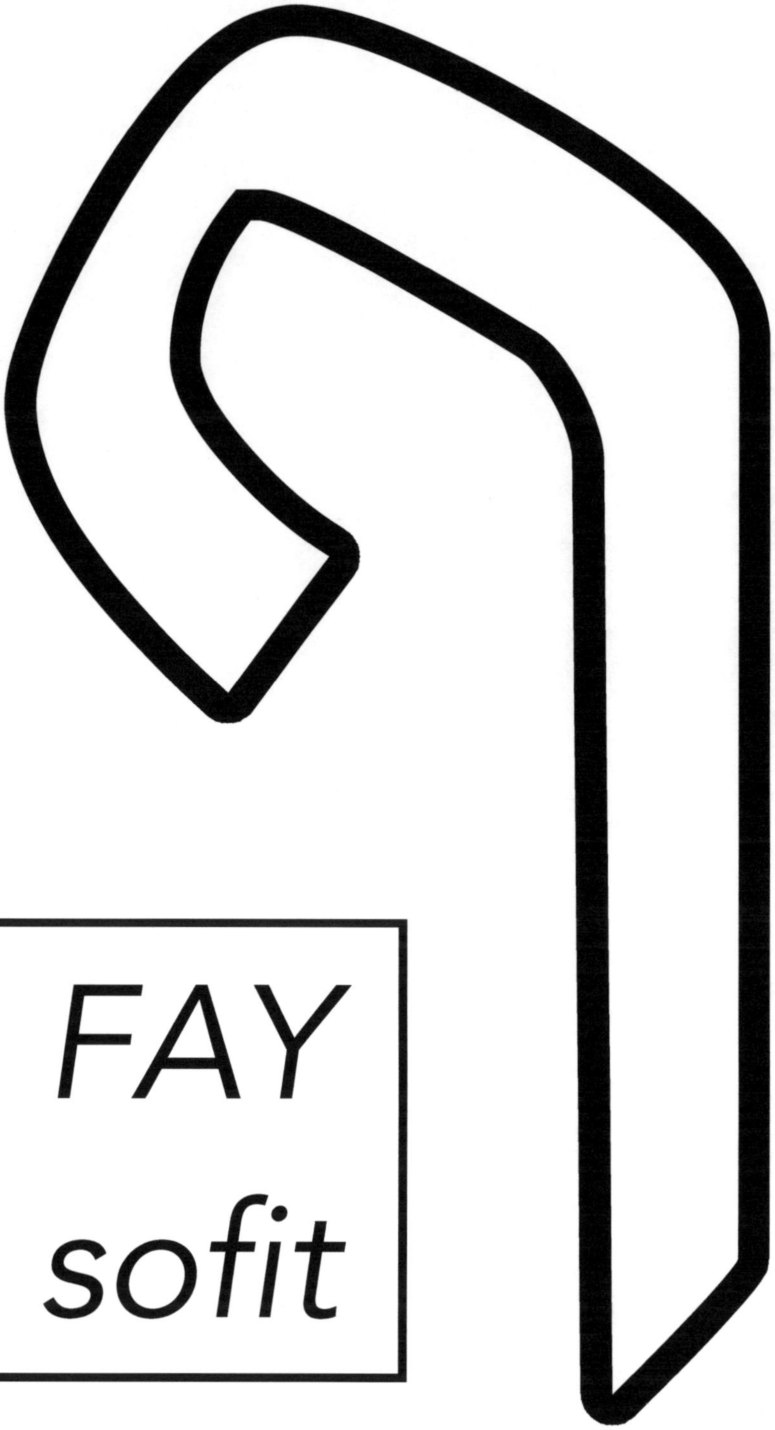

FAY
sofit

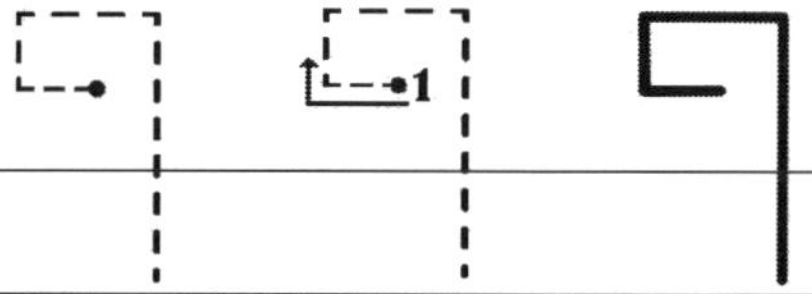

28   The Aleph Bet Coloring Book © 2017 Michelle Geft

א בב ג ד ה ו ז ח ט י כך ל מם נן ס ע פפף צץ ק ר שׁשׂ ת

THIS IS THE LETTER TZADI.
TZADI SAYS "TZ" AS IN RITZ.

The letter *Tzadi* represents the number ninety.

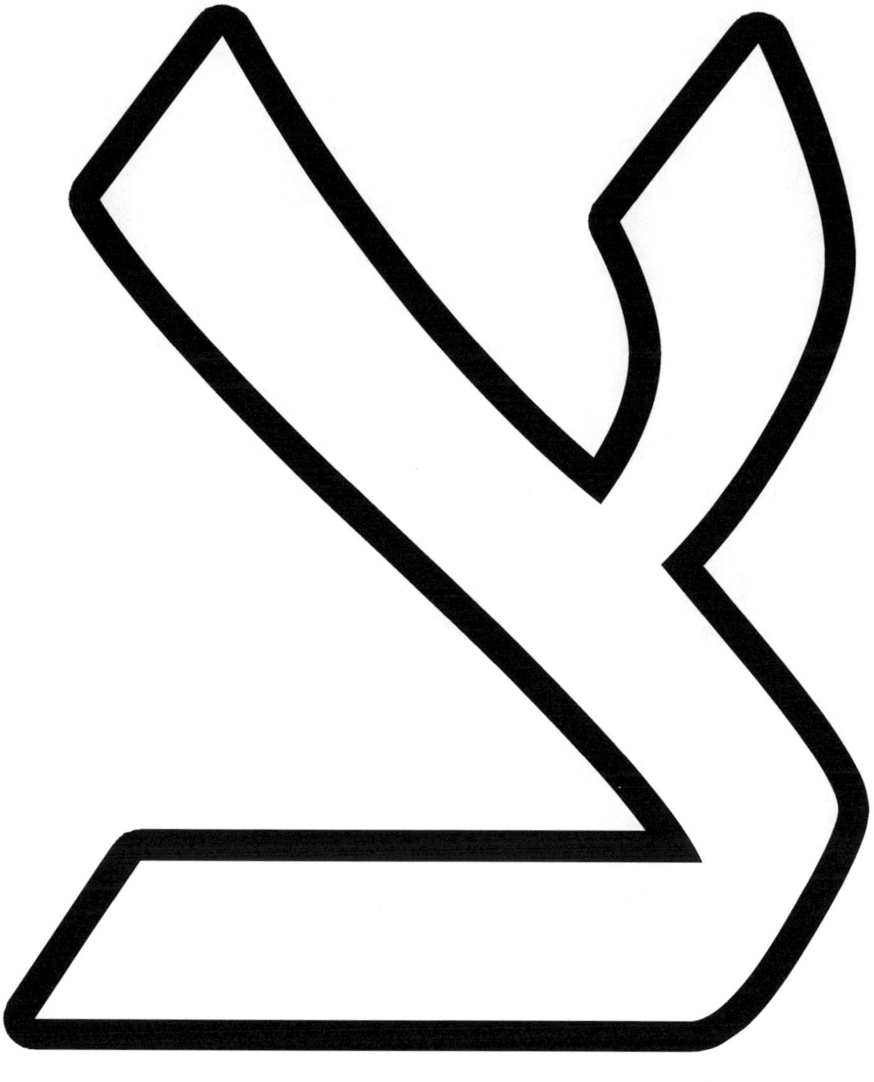

TZADI

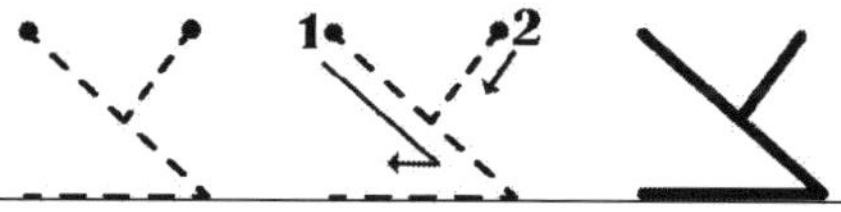

א אב ג ד ה ו ז ח ט י כךכ ל מם נן ס ע ףפפ ץצ ק ר שׁשׂ ת

THIS IS THE LETTER TZADI SOFIT.
TZADI SOFIT SAYS "TZ" AS IN RITZ.
Tzadi Sofit is only found at the end of a word
in place of the *Tzadi.* ✡

THE *TZADI SOFIT* DOES NOT TAKE VOWELS.

TZADI sofit

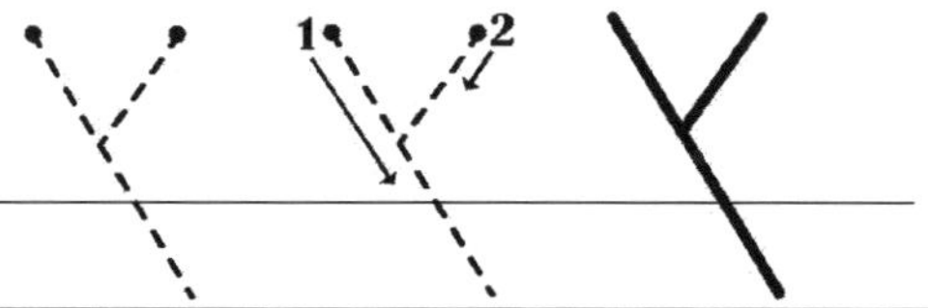

א ב ג ד ה ו ז ח ט י כך ל מ ס ע פ פף צץ ק ר ש ש ת

THIS IS THE LETTER KOOF (or KOF).
KOOF SAYS "K" AS IN KITE.

The letter *Koof* represents the number one hundred.

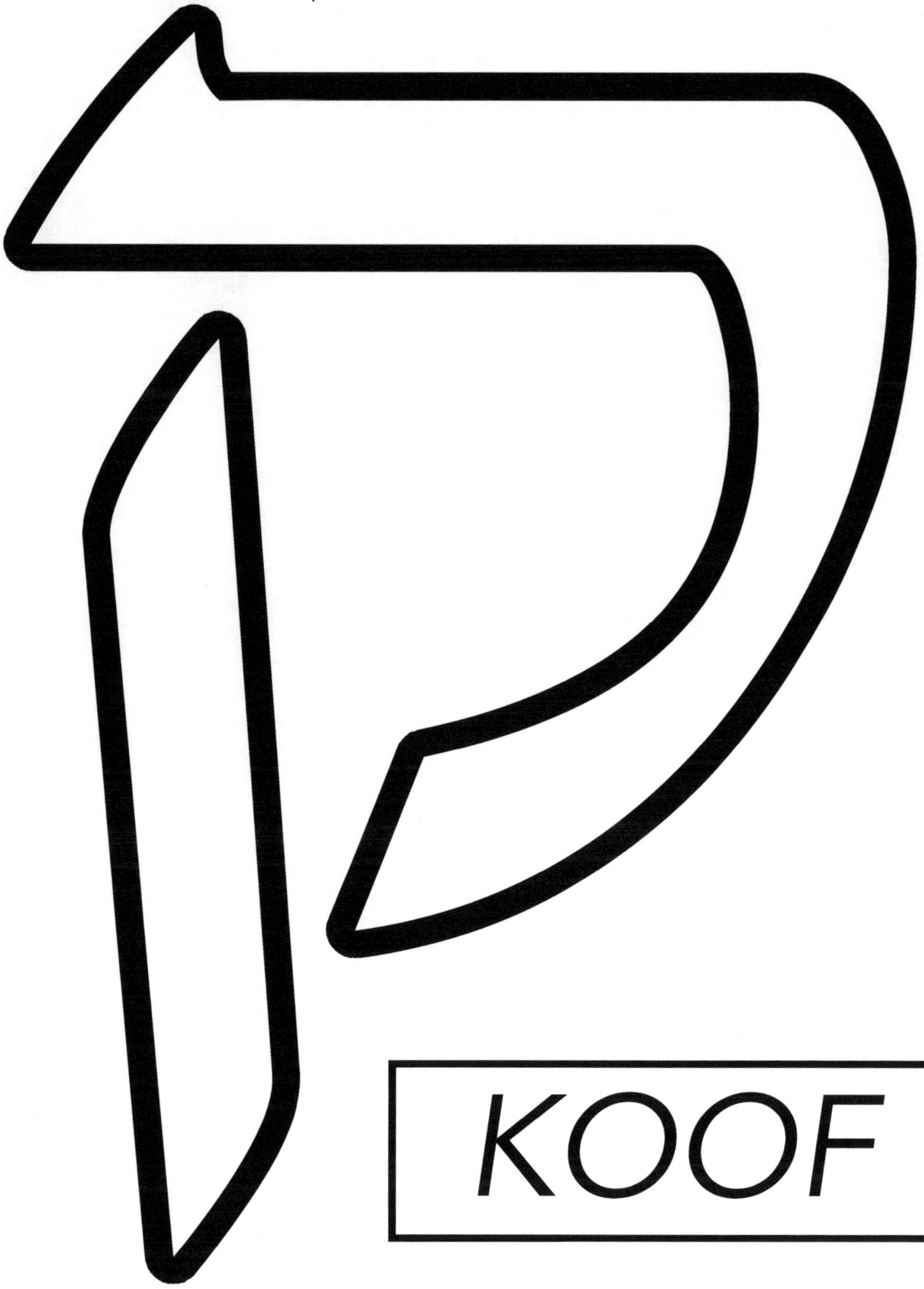

KOOF

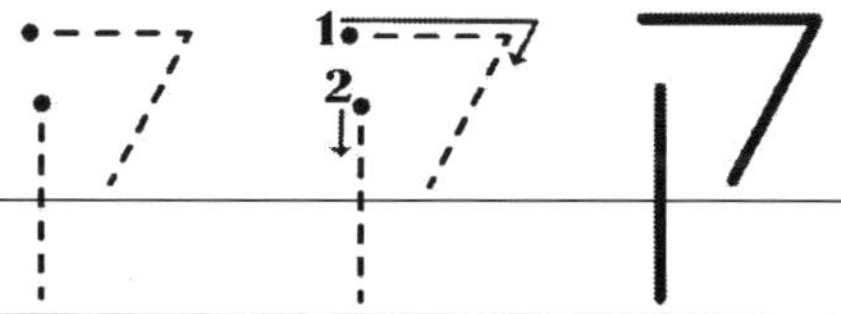

31   The Aleph Bet Coloring Book © 2017 Michelle Geft

א בב ג ד ה ו ז ח ט י ככך ל מם נן ס ע פפף צץ ק ר שש ת

THIS IS THE LETTER RESH.
RESH SAYS "R" AS IN RAIN.

The letter *Resh* represents the number two hundred.

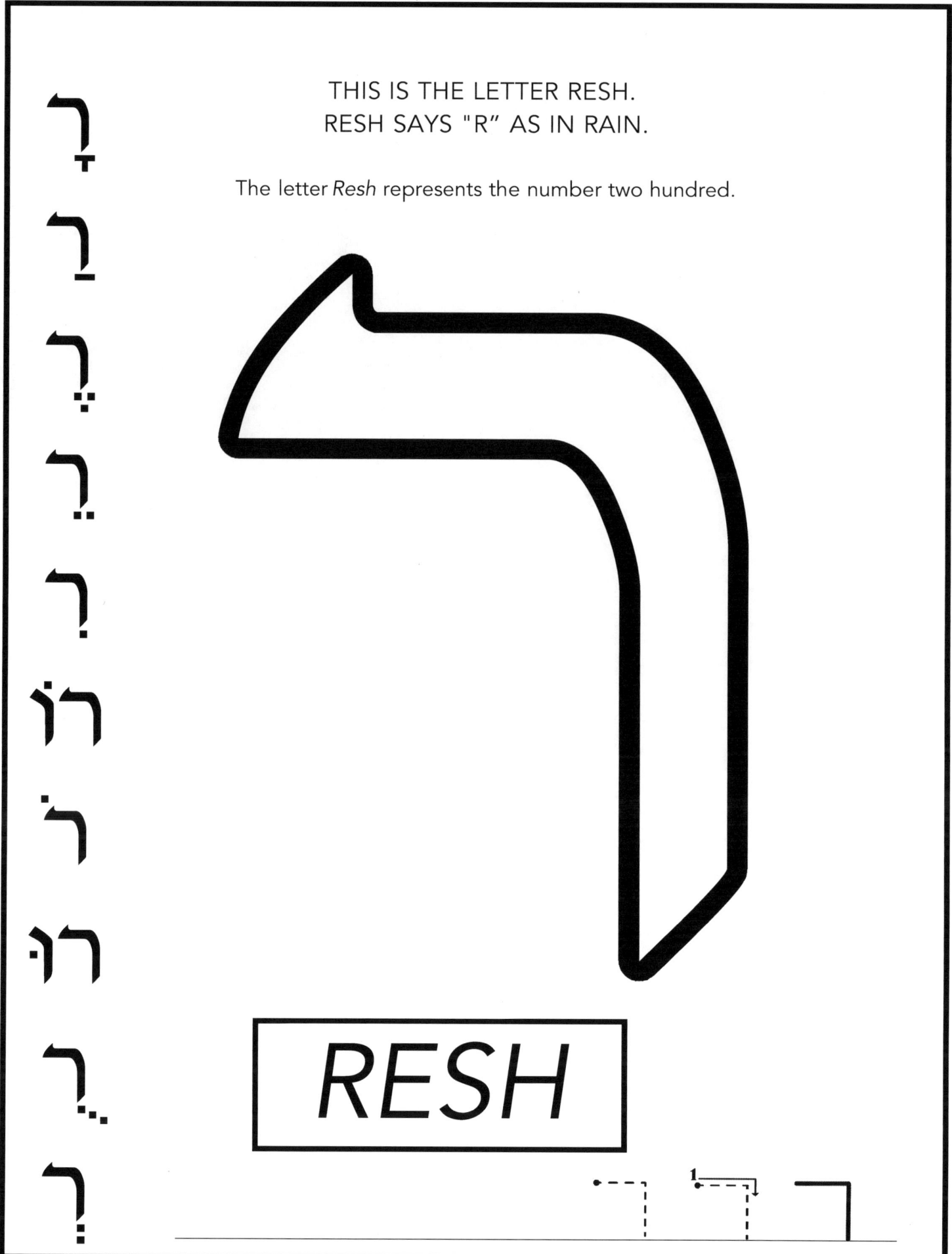

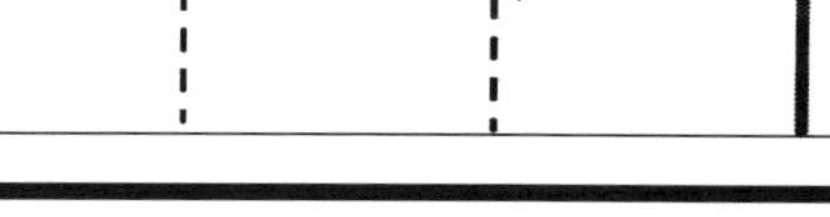

RESH

32 The Aleph Bet Coloring Book © 2017 Michelle Geft

אבגדהוזחטיכךלמםןןסעפףצץקרשׁשׂת

THIS IS THE LETTER SHIN.
SHIN SAYS "SH" AS IN SHOE.

The letter *Shin* represents the number three hundred.

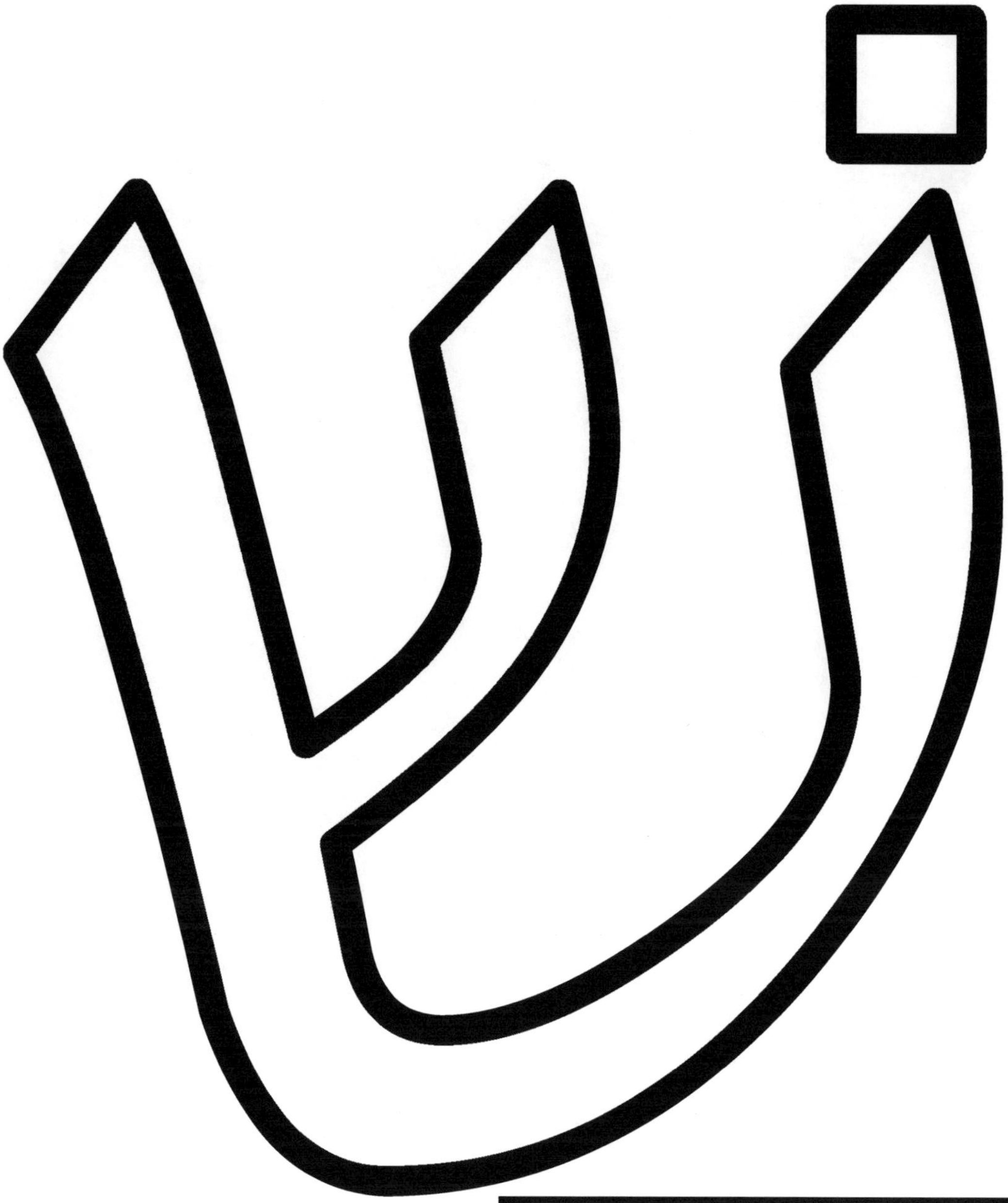

SHIN

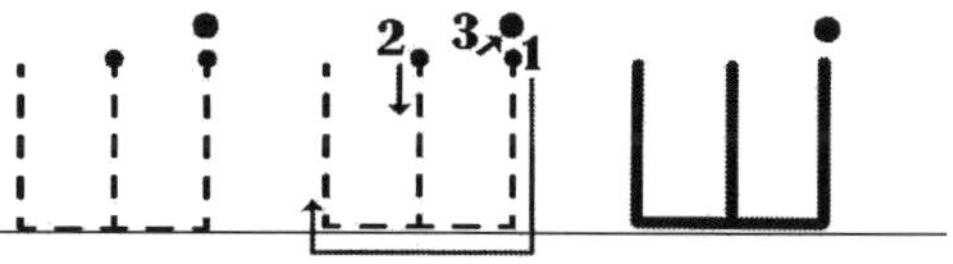

33   The Aleph Bet Coloring Book © 2017 Michelle Geft

א בב ג ד ה ו ז ח ט י כּכ ל מם נן ס ע פּפ צץ ק ר שׂש תּ

THIS IS THE LETTER SIN.
SIN SAYS "S" AS IN SUN.
The *Sin* is a version of the *Shin*.
Notice the dot moved from the upper right (in the *Shin*)
to the upper left (in the *Sin*).

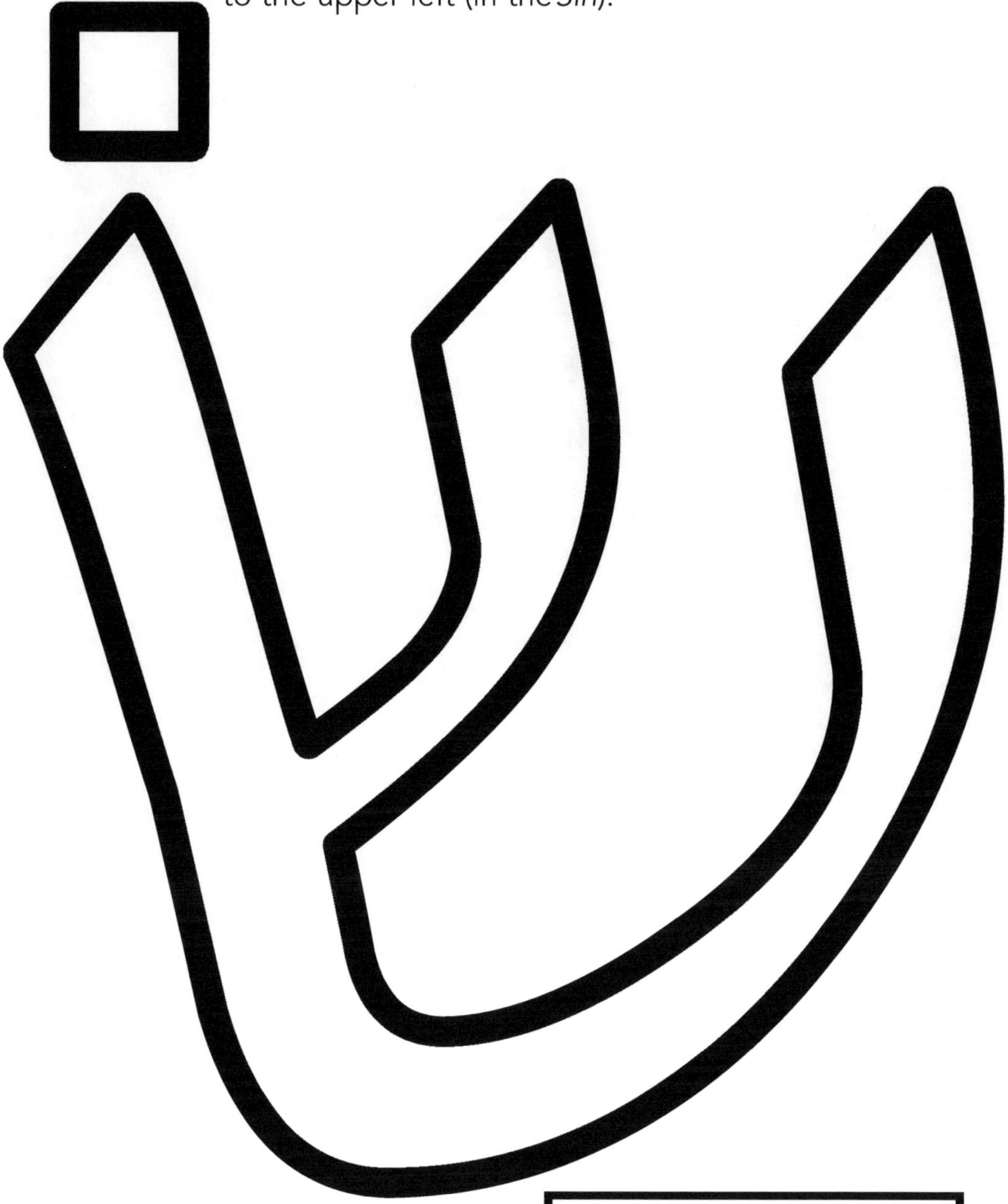

שָׂ
שֵׂ
שֶׂ
שִׂ
שׂוֹ
שֹׂ
שׂוּ
שֻׂ
שְׂ

SIN

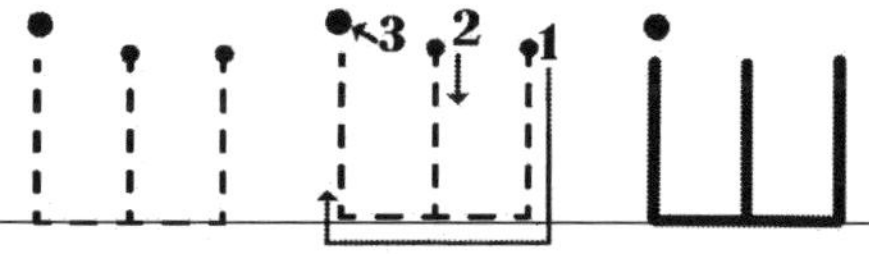

34 The Aleph Bet Coloring Book © 2017 Michelle Geft

א בב ג ד ה ו ז ח ט י כך ל מם נן ס ע פפף צץ ק ר שׁשׂ ת

THIS IS THE LETTER TAV.
TAV SAYS "T" AS IN TIME.
The *Tav* sometimes has a *dagesh* and in
modern Hebrew, they both say "t."

תּ / ת

The letter *Tav* represents the number four hundred.

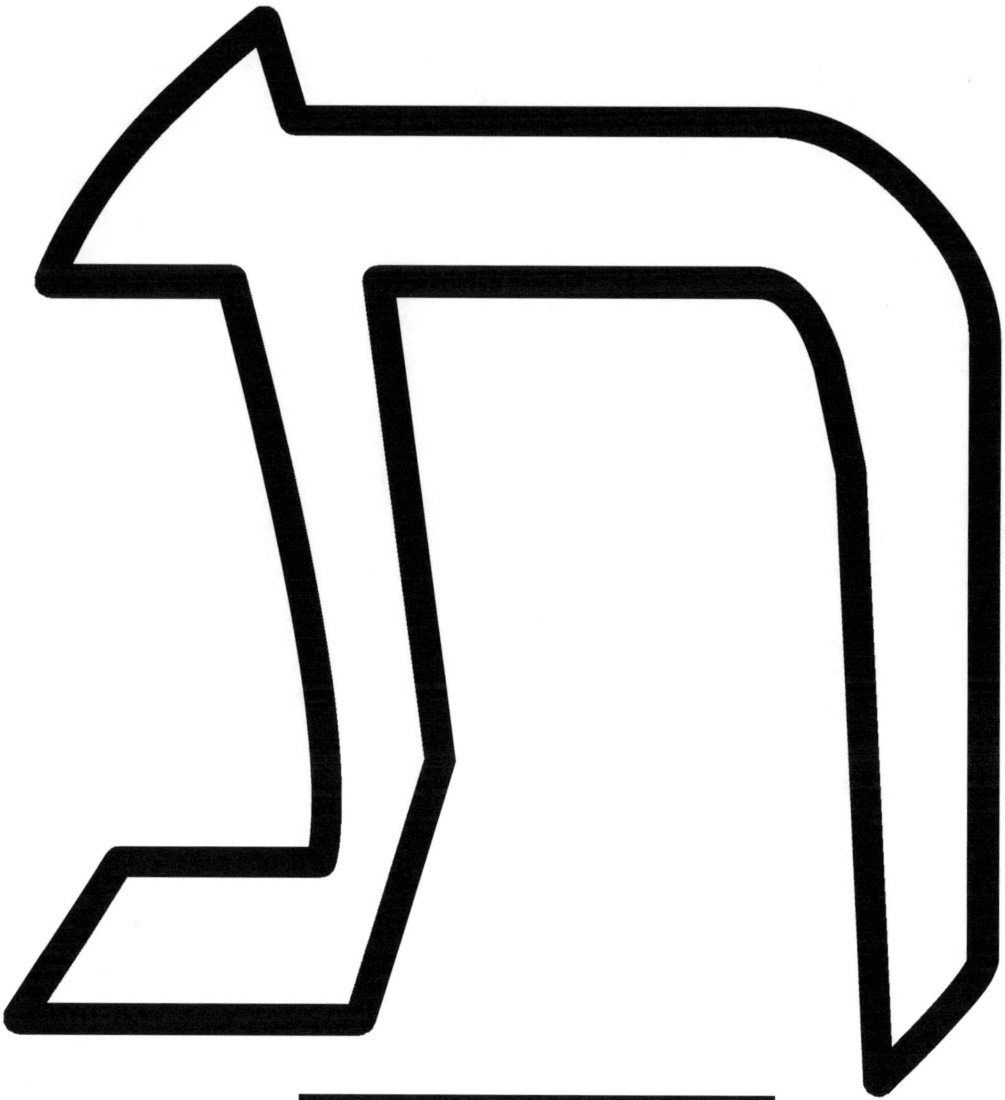

TAV

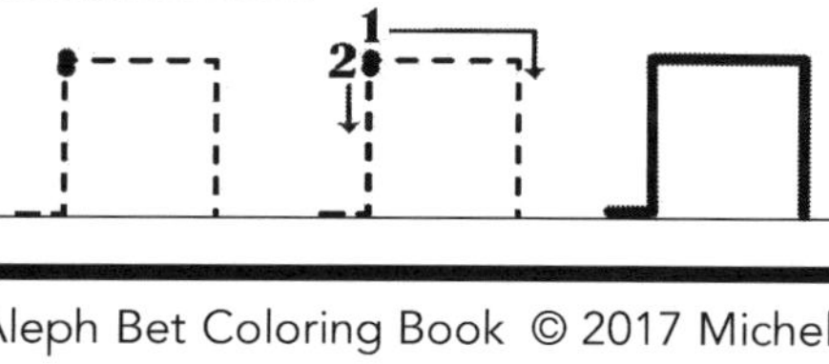

35   The Aleph Bet Coloring Book © 2017 Michelle Geft

Read and write the letters:

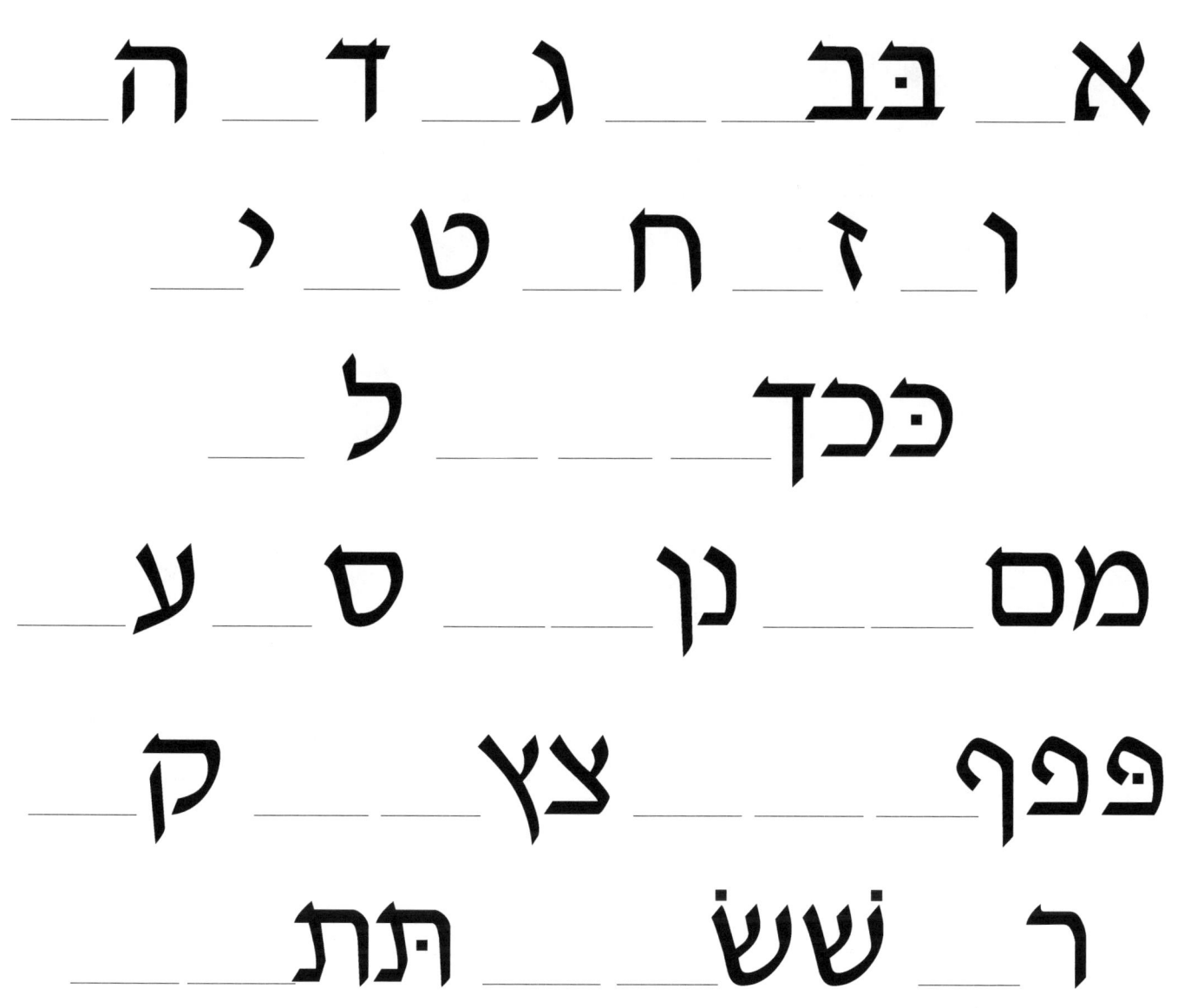

א בּב ___ ג ___ ד ___ ה ___

___ י ___ ט ח ___ ז ___ ו

כּכך ___ ___ ___ ___ ל ___

מם ___ נן ___ ס ___ ע ___

פּפף ___ ___ צץ ___ ק ___

ר שׁש ___ ___ תּת ___

Practice until you know every letter. ✡

Try to combine the letters and vowels you learned into words:

Common words / Phrases:

hello/goodbye/peace	shalom	שָׁלוֹם
excuse me/sorry	silee'ha	סְלִיחָה
please/you're welcome		בְּבַקָשָׁה*
thank you	toh'da	תּוֹדָה
thank you very much		תּוֹדָה רַבָּה**
see you later		לְהִתְרָאוֹת***
yes	ken	כֵּן
no	lo	לֹא
maybe	oo'lie	אוּלַי
to life! / cheers!	liha'yim	לְחַיִּים
here	po	פֹּה
there	sham	שָׁם
name	shem	שֵׁם
of	shel	שֶׁל
mine	she'lee	שֶׁלִי
good	tov	טוֹב
Hebrew	eev'reet	עִבְרִית
English	an'gleet	אַנְגְלִית

*biva'ka'sha, **toh'da ra'ba,
***liheet'ra'ot

Personal Pronouns:

I	a'ni	אֲנִי
you (m.s.)	a'ta	אַתָּה
you (f.s.)	at	אַתְּ
he	hoo	הוּא
she	hee	הִיא
we	a'nah'nu	אֲנַחְנוּ
you (m.p.)	a'tem	אַתֶּם
you (f.p.)	a'ten	אַתֶּן
they (m)	hem	הֵם
they (f)	hen	הֵן

Questions:

who	mee	מִי
what	ma	מַה/מָה
where (is)	ay'fo	אֵיפֹה
to where	lian	לְאָן
why	la'ma	לָמָה
why	ma'doo'ah	מַדוּעַ
when	ma'tai	מָתַי
how much	ka'ma	כַּמָה
how	ayh	אֵיךְ
which	ay'ze	אֵיזֶה
which	ay'zo	אֵיזוֹ
which (plural)	ay'loo	אֵילוּ

The Aleph Bet Coloring Book © 2017 Michelle Geft

You just learned the Aleph Bet in the printed form.
You will see Hebrew written like this in books, newspapers, street signs and anywhere else words are printed.

The Aleph Bet also has a handwritten form, a script form. If you continue your studies you will also learn to write and read Hebrew in this form.

Printed: א ב ג ד ה ו ז ח ט י כ ל מ נ ס ע פ צ ק ר ש ת

Script: אׄ ב ג ד ה ו ז ח ט י כׄ ל מ נ ס ע פ צ ק ר ש ת

If you would like to continue your studies in reading and writing Hebrew, find my other book:

Read, Write, Recite Hebrew
A Beginner's Guide to the Hebrew Alphabet

www.HebrewBasics.com

✂ Cut out a bookmark and put it to the left of the coloring book to help you read. ✂

ah	ah	ah	ah	ah
ah	ah	ah	ah	ah
eh	eh	eh	eh	eh
eh(ay)	eh(ay)	eh(ay)	eh(ay)	eh(ay)
ee	ee	ee	ee	ee
oh	oh	oh	oh	oh
oh	oh	oh	oh	oh
oo	oo	oo	oo	oo
oo	oo	oo	oo	oo
ih	ih	ih	ih	ih

The Aleph Bet Coloring Book ©2017 Michelle Geft

39   The Aleph Bet Coloring Book © 2017 Michelle Geft

48710020R00043

Made in the USA
Columbia, SC
08 December 2024